dBase III

A READY REFERENCE MANUAL

A READY REFERENCE MANUAL

CATHERINE GARRISON
MERCEDES A. McGOWEN
MARILYN K. POPYK

ADDISON-WESLEY PUBLISHING COMPANY, INC.
Reading, Massachusetts • Menlo Park, California • Don Mills, Ontario
Wokingham, England • Amsterdam • Sydney • Singapore • Tokyo
Madrid • Bogotá • Santiago • San Juan

This book was produced by Addison-Wesley using MicroTEX. The output was generated on an Apple Laser Writer.

First Printing, January 1987

Copyright ©1987 by Addison-Wesley Publishing Company, Inc.

All rights reserved. No part of this publication may be reproduced, stored in a retrieval system, or transmitted, in any form or by any means, electronic, mechanical, photocopying, recording, or otherwise, without the prior written permission of the publisher. Printed in the United States of America. Published simultaneously in Canada.

ISBN 0-201-11625-1
CDEFGHIJ-AL-8987

dBASE III is a registered trademark of Ashton-Tate Corporation.

The procedures and applications presented in this book have been included for their instructional value. They have been tested with care but are not guaranteed for any particular purpose. The publisher does not offer any warranties or representations, nor does it accept any liabilities with respect to the programs or applications.

Contents

INTRODUCTION TO dBASE III   **1**

What Is dBASE III?   1
Database Files   1
Database File Structure   2
Field Types   2
File Procedures   3
    Creating a File   3
    Working in a File   3
Scope of dBASE Commands   3
Other Kinds of dBASE III Files   4
    dBASE III File Types and Their File Extensions   4
Definitions   5
Limitations of dBASE III   7

ACCESSING dBASE III   **9**

Getting Started in dBASE   9
    On a Double Disk Drive System   9
    On a System with a Hard Disk   10
    Loading the Educational Version of dBASE III Plus   10

dBASE III BASICS   **11**

Basic Keys   11
Basic Commands   11
Using Basic Commands   12
dBASE Default Settings   12
    Viewing dBASE Default Settings and Disk Drive
        Information   13
    Changing a Default Setting   13
Status of Current dBASE Session   13
    Viewing Information about the Status of the Current
        Session of dBASE   13
    Printing the Current Status of the dBASE Work Session   13

CREATING FILES   15

Creating a Database File   15
    Creating a Database File Structure   15
    Ending Entry of Database File Structure and
        Remaining in dBASE   16
    Exiting dBASE and Returning to the Operating System   17
Creating Memo Fields in a Database File   17
    Creating a Memo Field in a File Structure   17
    Ending Entry of Memo Fields   18

ENTERING DATA   19

Adding Data   19
Adding Records to a Database File with APPEND   19
    Adding Data with APPEND and No Index Files in Use   20
    Adding Data to a Database File with APPEND and
        Index Files in Use in the Current Work Area   20
    Adding a Blank Record to the End of a Database File   20
Adding Records with BROWSE   21
    Adding a New Record to a Database File with BROWSE   21
Adding Records with the INSERT Command   21
    Inserting a New Record after the Current Record   21
    Inserting a New Record in a Database File before the
        Current Record   22
Inserting Blank Records   22
    Inserting a Blank Record in a Database File at the
        Current Record   22
    Inserting a Blank Record in a Database File before the
        Current Record   22
Adding Data to a Memo Field   22
    Adding Data to a Memo Field with APPEND   23

Adding Data to a Memo Field with BROWSE 23
Adding Data to a Memo Field with INSERT 23

SAVING FILES 25

Saving a File Structure 25
    Saving a Newly Created Database File Structure 25
Saving Data in APPEND 26
    Saving All Data Entered and Exiting APPEND from the Current Record 26
    Saving All Data Entered and Exiting APPEND from a Blank Record 26
    Saving All Data Entered Except That in the Current Record 26
Saving Data in INSERT 26
    Saving Data Added with the INSERT Command 26
    Exiting INSERT without Saving Newly Added Data 26
Saving Data in EDIT 27
    Saving Changes in the Record and Advancing One Record 27
    Saving Changes in the Record and Moving Back One Record 27
    Saving All Changes Made in the File and Exiting EDIT 27
    Exiting EDIT without Saving Changes Made in the Current Record 27
Saving Changes in BROWSE 27
    Saving Changes Made in BROWSE and Advancing to the Next Window 27
    Saving Changes Made in BROWSE and Moving Back One Window 27
    Saving All Changes and Exiting BROWSE 27
    Exiting BROWSE without Saving the Current Entry 28
    Exiting a Memo Field and Saving Newly Added Data 28
    Exiting a Memo Field without Saving Newly Added Data 28

VIEWING DATA 29

Viewing Options 29
Adjusting the Pointer 29
Viewing an Existing Database File 30
Viewing Records of a Database File 30
    Viewing All Records with Screen Scrolling 31
    Viewing All Records One Screen at a Time 31
    Viewing the First Record 31
    Viewing the Last Record 31
    Viewing a Specific Record 31
    Viewing Records by a Specific Date 32

Viewing Data Using Logical Operators .AND., .OR., and .NOT.   32
    Viewing Records Using .AND.   32
    Viewing Records Using .OR.   32
    Viewing Records Using .NOT.   33
Viewing Data Using Relational Operators $>, <, =, <>$ 33
    Viewing Records That Are Greater Than a Specified Value   33
    Viewing Records That Are Greater Than or Equal to a Specified Value   33
    Viewing Records That Are Less Than a Specified Value   33
    Viewing Records That Are Less Than or Equal to a Specified Value   34
    Viewing Records That Are Not Equal to a Specified Numeric Value   34
    Viewing Records That Are Not Equal to a Specified Character Value   34
Viewing Records with or without Record Numbers   34
    Viewing All Records with No Record Numbers Displayed   34
    Viewing Specific Fields with Record Numbers   35
    Viewing Specific Fields without Record Numbers   35
    Viewing Only Records for Which the Command Expression Is True   35
Viewing Records in a Database File That Is Already In Use   35
    Viewing the First Record   35
    Viewing a Record Following the Last One Displayed in the Database File   36
    Viewing a Record Which Preceeds the Last One Displayed in the Database File   3

CHANGING DATA   37

Commands That Change Data   37
Moving the Cursor Using EDIT or BROWSE   37
    Moving the Cursor Down One Field   37
    Moving the Cursor Back to the Previous Field   38
    Moving the Cursor to the Right One Character   38
    Moving the Cursor to the Left One Character   38
    Moving the Cursor One Word to the Right   38
    Moving the Cursor One Word to the Left   38
Inserting Data   38
    Inserting a New Line or Field Definition   38
Deleting Characters   38

      Deleting the Character at the Cursor   38
      Deleting the Character to the Left of the Cursor   38
      Deleting One Word to the Right of the Cursor Position   38
      Deleting Data to the End of the Field   39
Marking and Unmarking Records for Deletion   39
    Marking a Record for Deletion   39
    Removing the Deletion Mark from a Record   39
Editing Data   39
    Changing Data in a Database Record using the
        EDIT Command   39
    Changing from EDIT (Overwrite Mode) to INSERT
        (Insert Mode)   39
Browsing a Database File   40
    Changing Data Using the BROWSE Command   40
    Moving the Display Window One Field to the Right   40
    Moving the Display Window One Field to the Left   40
    Moving the Display Window Down   40
    Moving the Display Window Up   40

REARRANGING DATA   41

INDEX and SORT Comparisons   41
Sorting Files   42
    Sorting a File   43
    Sorting a Database File without Differentiating
        Upper or Lower Case   43
    Sorting a Database File on Descending Order   43
    Sorting on a Date Field (Latest to Earliest)   43
    Sorting on More Than One Field of the Same Type   44
Indexing Files   44
    Indexing on a Character Field Type   44
    Indexing on Numeric Fields   45
    Indexing on a Date Field (Earliest to Latest)   45
    Indexing on a Date Field (Latest to Earliest)   45
    Indexing on More Than One Field of the Same Type   45
    Indexing on Two Fields That Are Not of the Same Type   45
Indexing in Descending Order   46
    When the Key Field Is a Character Type   46
    When the Key Field Is Numeric   46

LOCATING DATA

Locating Information   47
Finding Information Using LOCATE   47
    Locating Records Based on the First Data Character   48
    Locating Records for a Specified Field .AND. Date   48
    Locating Records for a Specified Field .OR. Date   48
    Locating Specific Data Contained in Records in the File   49
Finding Information in an Indexed File   49
Locating Information Using FIND   49
    Finding Records Based on the First Field Character   49
    Finding a Record Using an Indexed File   50
    Finding a Record Using a Different Index File   50
    Finding Several Records   50
    Finding Records Using a Combined Index of More
        Than One Field   51
Locating Information Using SEEK   51
    Finding Data Indexed on a Date Field   51

DELETING DATA   53

Removing Records   53
Marking Records for Deletion   54
    Marking a Record for Deletion   54
    Marking Specified Records for Deletion by Field   54
    Marking Specified Records for Deletion by Date   54
    Marking the Next Record(s) after the Current
        Record for Deletion   54
Unmarking Records Previously Marked for Deletion   55
    Unmarking a Record for Deletion in a Database File   55
    Unmarking All Records Marked for Deletion   55
    Unmarking Only the First Record Marked for Deletion   55
    Unmarking Specified Records Marked for Deletion   55
    Unmarking Records Specified by Date Marked for Deletion   56
Removing Records Marked for Deletion   56
    Removing All Records Previously Marked for Deletion   56
    Removing a Specified Record That Has Previously
        Been Marked for Deletion   56
Removing All Records from a Database File   56
    Removing All Records from a Database File Using ZAP   57
    Removing All Records Using PACK   57
Removing Files   57
    Removing a File   57
Deleting Data While in EDIT or BROWSE Mode   57
    Marking a Record for Deletion   58

Removing the Deletion Mark from a Record   58
Removing Records Marked for Deletion and No
    Active Index Files   58
Deleting Information in a Field While in EDIT or BROWSE   58
Deleting the Character at the Cursor   58
Deleting the Character to the Left of the Cursor   58
Deleting One Word to the Right of the Cursor   58
Deleting Data to the End of the Field   58

GLOBAL CHANGES   59

Using Global File Commands   59
Replacing Records in a Database File   59
    Replacing One Field in All Records of the Database File   60
    Replacing One Field in One Record in a Database File   60
    Replacing One Field in Specified Records in a Database File   60
    Replacing the Date Field for One Record in the
        Database File   60
    Replacing Selected Records for a Given Field of the
        Database File   61
    Replacing the Value of a Selected Record for a Given Field   61
Changing Specified Fields and Records   61
    Editing Specified Fields and Records   61
Updating Index Files   62
    Opening Index Files before Changing the Database File   62
    Updating an Index File When Data Are Replaced
        in One Field   62
    Removing All Records Marked for Deletion in a Database
        File   62
    Removing All Records from the Active Database File (including
        those NOT marked for deletion)   63

FILE MANAGEMENT   65

File Structure Commands   65
    Viewing the Structure of a File   65
    Copying the File Structure   65
    Modifying the File Structure   66
    Changing the Structure of a File   66
    Exiting MODIFY STRUCTURE without Saving Changes   66
    Printing the Structure of the File   67
Database File Commands   67
    Using Files   67
    Using a Database File   67

xi

      Using One Index File with a Database File   67
      Using Multiple Index Files with a Database File   67
   Viewing Files   67
      Viewing the Contents of a Database File   67
      Viewing the Names of Files on the Default Disk Drive   68
      Viewing the Names of Data Files on Another Disk Drive   68
      Viewing Specific Types of Files on a Given Disk Drive   68
      Viewing All Files of All Types on a Given Disk Drive   68
   Copying Files   69
      Copying a Database File   69
      Copying Specified Fields to a New Database File   69
      Copying Fields That Match Specified Data   69
      Copying All Types of Files, Including Database Files   69
   Renaming Files in dBASE   70
      Renaming a File on the Default Drive   70
      Renaming a File on a Drive Other Than the Default Drive   70
   Removing Files from a Directory While in dBASE   70
      Removing a File from the Directory   70
   Closing Files and Remaining in dBASE   70
      Closing a Database File Currently in Use   70
      Closing All Open Index Files of a Database File in Use   70
      Closing All Open Database, Index, and Format Files   71
   Closing Files and Exiting dBASE   71
      Closing All Open Files and Returning to the
         Operation System   71
   Text File Commands   71
      Viewing Contents of a Text File   71
      Printing Contents of a Text File   71

COMPUTATION IN dBASE   73

Using Math Functions   73
Counting Records   73
   Using COUNT to Determine the Number of Records
      That Meet Specified Conditions   74
USING SUM   74
   Using SUM to Total the Contents of One Field   74
   Using SUM to Total the Contents of Several Fields   74
   Using SUM to Add the Contents of Two Combined Fields   74
   Using SUM to Calculate Total Price   74
   Using SUM to Calculate the Subtotal Cost of
      Specified Records   75
   Using SUM to Calculate the Subtotal for a Given Date   75

    Using SUM to Calculate Totals on Fields Greater Than a
        Specified Amount   75
    Using SUM to Calculate Totals after a Given Date   76
Using TOTAL   76
    Using TOTAL to Calculate Subtotals   76
    Viewing Totals for Several Fields   77
Using AVERAGE   77
    Using AVERAGE to Average Numeric Fields   77

REPORTS   79

Generating Reports   79
    Default Settings for Reports   80
    Creating a Report   80
    Exiting CREATE REPORT   81
Creating Reports with Totals   81
    Creating a Report with Subtotals on a Field   81
    Viewing a Report   82
    Viewing Selected Records in a Report   82
    Rearranging Data in a Report Usng an Indexed File   82
    Changing Data in a Report File   82
    Inserting Spaces in Front of a Report Column Heading   82
    Printing Reports   83

MULTIPLE FILES   85

Multiple Files in dBASE III   85
    Using Multiple Files   86
    Moving between Open Database Files   86
    Retrieving Data from Both Databases Simultaneously   86
Closing Multiple Open Database Files   87

CONVERTING FILES   89

File Conversion   89
    Converting a dBASE III File for Use with WordStar   89
    Converting a dBASE III File for Use with MailMerge   90
    Converting a dBASE III File for Use with SuperCalc3   90
    Converting a dBASE III File for Use with Lotus 1-2-3   90
Importing Files into dBASE III   91
    Importing Files from WordStar   91
    Importing Files from Lotus 1-2-3   91
    Translating a Lotus 1-2-3 File   91

USING FUNCTION KEYS   93

Function Keys   93
Function Key Assignments   93
Reprogramming a Function Key   94
Changing a Function Key Permanently   94

NEW FEATURES OF dBASE III PLUS   95

Changes and New Features of dBASE III Plus   95
    Escaping The Assistant to the Dot Prompt   95
New Commands   95
New Numeric Functions   96
New Functions   96
New String Functions   97

THE ASSISTANT   99

Using The Assistant   99
Entering dBASE III Plus   99
Features of The Assistant Display   100
    Top Portion of the Screen Display Consists of   100
    Bottom Portion of the Screen Display Consists of   100
Using Menus   100
    Opening the Selected Menu   100
    Selecting Menu Options   101
    Selecting Submenu Options   101
    Canceling Selections   101
Exiting The Assistant   101
    Escaping The Assistant to the Dot Prompt of dBASE III Plus   101
    Returning to The Assistant from the Dot Prompt   102
    Quitting dBASE III Plus from The Assistant   102
Converting Files   102
    Conversion of dBASE III Plus Files to pfs:File Files   102
    Conversion of pfs:File Files to dBASE III Plus Files   102
The Query Option   102
View Files   103

Introduction

Why purchase this book? Because you will learn to use dBASE III faster if you can look up the action you wish to perform. For about the price of a fast-food dinner for two, you can own a convenient summary of dBASE III procedures. Long after dinner would be digested, the Ready Reference manual will still be there to assist you.

Want to know a little more about the Ready Reference Manual? It is a convenient summary of commonly used dBASE III procedures and commands, designed to assist you in performing common database management tasks. Unlike most manuals, it is organized by function, rather than by command. This enables you to find the action you need to perform without knowing the specific commands used in the procedure.

Like most manuals, this guide is intended to act as a reference tool. For a complete introduction to and definition of database concepts, you should read the database chapters in Marilyn Popyk's *Up and Running! MicroComputer Applications* before beginning to use dBASE III.

Important Instructions for Users of the Educational Version

An educational version of dBASE III PLUS is available with Marilyn Popyk's *Up and Running! MicroComputer Applications*. This version of dBASE III PLUS will permit you to do almost everything that you could do with the regular version. However, you should know the following facts about the educational version.

1. Files cannot exceed 31 records.
2. Up to 10 database files can be opened at once.
3. The educational version of dBASE III PLUS requires a 256K IBM PC or compatible with two disk drives or a hard disk. With DOS 3.0 or higher, 384K of memory is required.

dBASE III PLUS allows the flexibility of using dBASE III dot commands of The Assistant, a fully menu-driven user interface. This Ready Reference Manual focuses on the dot commands before providing an overview of dBASE III PLUS and The Assistant. To use this manual with the educational version of dBASE II PLUS, load the dBASE III PLUS software and then press ESC to access the dot commands.

Introduction to dBASE III

What Is dBASE III?

dBASE III is an integrated computerized file system that manages information. Information is organized and stored in files that can be accessed easily from other files. dBASE III has the following functions:

Data entry: Information (data) can be entered, added, changed, rearranged, deleted, and viewed.

Queries: Specified parts of the stored information can be located, looked at, and analyzed.

Report Generation: Stored data can be summarized, analyzed, and printed.

DATABASE FILES

Information is stored in files that consist of groups of records made up of individual pieces of information called fields.
   The database file has two parts:

File Structure: A list of fields that indicate the kinds of information stored in the file.

Records: Fields of the stored data.

DATABASE FILE STRUCTURE

Think of a tabular chart of rows and columns. The file is the tabular chart, the records are the rows, and the columns are the fields of the database file. The database file structure consists of the following:

Filename: Not more than eight characters and no spaces (may be followed by an optional period and three-letter file extension).

Fieldname: Not more than ten characters and no spaces.

Field Type: Indicates the kind of information stored in the field.

Field Width: Indicates the size (number of characters) of the field.

Decimal: Indicates the number of decimal places to the right of the decimal point.

FIELD TYPES

The computer makes distinctions between character and numeric information. dBASE III defines five types of information: character, numeric, date, memo, and logical. The user is required to state what type of information is to be stored in each field.

Character (C): Any data (character or numeric) not used for numeric computation are considered character data.

The first character must be alphabetical.
Character field type data are left-justified.
Data that consist of numbers on which computation is NOT performed will be entered as (C) character data, especially if the data include hyphens or any alphabetical characters.
Zipcodes are examples of data that can include hyphens and alphabetical characters. Zipcodes are character field types (C).

Numeric (N): Numeric data that are used in computations are the only data used in a numeric field.

No alphabetical characters are used in a numeric field.
Numeric type data are right-justified.

Logical (L): A logical field contains a one character true or false value.

Responses to queries about logical fields include Y, y, T, and t for True # statements; N, n, F, and f for False statements.

Date (D): Dates are entered and displayed in the form MM/DD/YY.

dBASE III stores dates as a single number YYYYMMDD. Later dates are larger than earlier dates, thus permitting computation and comparisons to be performed. (Julian date—the number of days since 01/01/01 A.D.) The width of the date field is eight characters.

Memo (M): A memo field is used for a document or text up to 4000 characters long (maximum length of one record).

A field that is to contain comments, a summary, or text should be designated a memo field if the number of characters exceeds 50.

FILE PROCEDURES

Creating a File

You get started using dBASE III by creating database files. The procedure to create a file is:

1. Create the file structure.
2. Enter data, record by record.
3. Save the entered data.
4. Close the database file.

Working in a File

Once database files are created, a file must be in USE or open before you can add, edit, rearrange, mark records for deletion, or remove records from the file.

Any changes or additions to the file must be saved in order to have the changes written to disk.

The file must be closed when all work on the database file is completed and changes or additions are saved. You have the option of remaining in dBASE to open and work on other files or to exit dBASE and return to the operating system.

The procedure for working on a database file can be summarized as follows:

1. Open (USE) the database file.
2. Enter, add, edit, delete, rearrange the data.
3. Save the modified database file.
4. Close the file.

SCOPE OF dBASE COMMANDS

Scope specifies what part of the database file the command applies to. Scope qualifiers are ALL, NEXT n, and FOR fieldname = 'data to be matched'.

What records are affected by dBASE III commands depends upon the scope of the command.

The command can apply to:

- only the current record;
- all records in the database file;
- the next n records following the current record;
- certain specified records, depending on how the command is worded.

Without a scope qualifier, the command defaults to the current record or the command applies to all records.

Commands that have a scope include AVERAGE, CHANGE, COPY TO, COUNT, DELETE, DISPLAY, LIST, LOCATE, RECALL, REPLACE, SUM, and TOTAL.

OTHER KINDS OF dBASE III FILES

In addition to the database file, dBASE III has several other kinds of files. All dBASE files consist of the filename and the file extension. The **file extension** is a three-letter abbreviation preceded by a period after the file name.

dBASE III File Types and Their File Extensions

Database file (.dbf): The basic file used to store data in records and fields.

Format file (.fmt): A file that generates custom screens for data entry and printed output.

Memo file (.dbt): A file that is used to store the contents of a memo field.

Index file (.ndx): A logical (alphabetical, chronological, or numerical) ordered file keyed to the record numbers of the database file.

Report form file (.frm): The file that contains the data used to prepare a report

Memory file (.mem): A file that is used to store variable values for later use.

Label file (.lbl)6: A file in which data needed to print labels are stored.

Command file (.cmd): A dBASE program

Text file (.txt): ASCII files of other purchased software programs that are able to be read into a dBASE III database file or dBASE files converted to ASCII format.

DEFINITIONS

The following terms are used in this guide and in most texts published for dBASE III:

Active file: The database file in USE in the currently selected work area. As many as ten files may be open at the same time. Each open file is assigned a work area in memory by dBASE III. A work area is SELECTed as the active work area in which normal database operations can be performed. Records of the file in the active work can be selected and altered. Records of other open files can be read only.

Ascending order: Ranking from lowest to highest (A to Z or 0 to 9).

ASCII: American Standard Code for Information Interchange, which defines the 128 standard characters used in computer programs. The characters include alphabetical and numerical characters, control characters, and symbols.

Current record: The record in the file currently in USE at which the record pointer is positioned.

Database: A collection of facts (data) that are systematically organized for central access, retrieval, and editing.

Database Management System (dbms:) A computerized system that integrates the data and makes access to the stored information easier.

Field: A single item of information within a record. Each item of information within a record is a separate field or column. Unique (key) fields (such as a Social Security number) are used as identifiers when retrieving data.

Field type: Designates the type of data that may be stored within the field: character, numeric, date, memo, or logical.

File: A collection of information about the same subject. A database file contains data in records made up of fields.

Index file: A file in which records are logically ordered by record number according to an item or items (field) of interest (key). Indexed files are in ascending order.

Key field: The field or expression by which a database file is indexed, totaled, updated, or joined to another database file. Indexes can be created on multiple key fields.

Query: A keyboard request for information based on data stored in the database file or other dBASE files.

Random search: A search in which not every record is compared. The assumption is made that the records are already ordered in some form.

Record: A unit of information within the file, a row, made up of items (fields or columns) of information.

In a file named CUSTOMERS, one record might consist of the following items of information that relate to a single customer, John Baker: Customer Name, Social Security Number, Street Address, City, State, Zipcode, Work Phone Number, Home Phone Number.

Record pointer: A number used by dBASE III to identify the current database record.

Relational database: One or more files viewed as tables of rows and columns. Each table is a **relation**. The rows are the records, and the columns are the fields of individual pieces of information. The files (or relations) are linked by common fields called keys.

Relational database management system: A computerized system that has the capability to cross reference relations (database files) by linking common fields within the different database files.

Scope: The part of the command that specifies which parts of the database file are to be affected by the command.

Sequential search: A search that begins with the first record and continues, record by record, until a match is found or the end of the file is reached.

Toggle: The same command is used to "turn on" or "turn off" some functions.

LIMITATIONS OF dBASE III

Character Use Restrictions

The maximum number of characters and the restrictions on character use are as follows:

Filename:	Eight characters; the first character must be a letter, and the file name may contain letters, numbers, and underscores. No embedded blank spaces are permitted.
Fieldname:	Ten characters; the first character must be a letter. Field names may contain letters, numbers and underscores. No embedded blank spaces are permitted.
Characters/record:	4000
Characters/field:	254
Characters/command line:	254
Characters/report heading:	254
Number of fields/record (maximum):	128
Number of records/database file:	1 billion
Number of files (all types) open simultaneously:	15
Number of database files open simultaneously: *Note:* A database file counts as two open files if memo fields are used.	10
Number of index files open per active database:	7
Number of format files open per active database:	1
Accuracy of numeric fields:	15.9 digits

Accessing dBASE III

GETTING STARTED IN dBASE

dBASE III is a program that can be used directly or by menu-driven systems. The user types in commands at the dot (.) prompt when working directly in dBASE. Some dBASE entries are selected from screen options that you choose by pressing the RETURN key or typing in your own data. On either a double disk drive or hard disk system you have the option of starting work or typing F1 and pressing RETURN to display the Menu of Help options at the dot (.) prompt.

On a Double Disk Drive System

dBASE III is normally used in disk drive A. Your data files are maintained on a separate disk, which is used in disk drive B.

1. Insert the operating system in disk drive A and, turn on the computer. (This boots the system.)
2. If prompted for the time and date, either enter RETURN to use the time and date shown or enter new values.
3. When the operating system prompt >A appears, remove the operating system disk and insert the dBASE III system disk.
4. Type DBASE and press RETURN.

5. Type SET DEFAULT TO B: and press RETURN when the dot prompt (.) appears. All data and program files are now directed to disk drive B. You are now ready to begin work in dBASE III.
6. Make frequent backup copies of all data files.

On a System with a Hard Disk

All dBASE III files are stored on the hard disk C. Your data files may be maintained on a floppy disk used in disk drive A, or they may be maintained on the hard disk C. The dBASE III program should be installed on the hard disk C.

1. Turn on the computer.
2. Type DBASE when the operating system prompt >C appears.
3. Type SET DEFAULT TO A: and press RETURN when the dot (.) prompt appears. All dBASE files created will be stored and retrieved from Disk drive A. You are ready to begin work in dBASE III.
4. Make frequent backup copies of all files.

Loading the Educational Version of dBase III PLUS

1. Insert the operating system in disk drive A and turn on the computer.
2. If prompted for the time and date, either enter RETURN or use the time and date shown or enter new values.
3. When the operating system prompt A appears, remove the operating system disk and insert disk 1 of dBASE PLUS.
4. Type DBASE and press RETURN.
5. When prompted, remove disk 1, insert disk 2 of dBASE PLUS and press return.
6. To access the dot command press ESC. You are now ready to begin work in dBASE III PLUS. All data files are automatically directed to disk drive B.

dBASE III Basics

BASIC KEYS

There are certain commands that are used most of the time you are working in dBASE. The RETURN key will be pressed after each dBASE command is entered. The CONTROL and ESCAPE keys are used frequently. dBASE III uses combinations of keys for many commands, such as pressing the CONTROL key followed by the letter Q. The notation for use of keys in commands varies from text to text. Common notation includes:

RETURN: RETURN, <RET>, ENTER, <return>, <cr>, or the right angle arrow on the IBM keyboard.

CONTROL Q: CTRL Q, ^Q, [CTRL/], [CTRL/q]

ESCAPE: ESC, <ESC>

In all cases, press the key or key combination indicated.

BASIC COMMANDS

dBASE III commands are one word commands. The command states what action will take place when the command is issued. Some of the basic commands needed to work with dBASE III are:

USE: Opens a database file so that you can add, edit, rearrange, or delete information in the file.

DISPLAY: Displays the current record on the screen.

DISPLAY ALL: Displays all the records in the database file, one screen at a time. To see additional records, press RETURN.

DISPLAY STRUCTURE: Displays the list of fields of the database file.

LIST: Displays all the records of a database file by scrolling them on the screen.

LIST STRUCTURE: Displays the list of fields of the database file, the field type, and the size of the field. This command is equivalent to DISPLAY STRUCTURE.

QUIT: Closes all open files and exits dBASE back to the operating system. Always QUIT dBASE before exiting to the operating system to prevent damage to open files and loss of data.

USING BASIC COMMANDS

A database management system is designed to work with files stored on floppy disks or on a hard disk instead of in file drawers. Instead of opening a file drawer, you open a file in dBASE by typing USE whenever you want to work with a new file.

When you USE dBASE files, you will frequently want to see what the records in the file look like. The results of a command are *not* displayed on the screen until you issue a command to view the results, except when you are in the EDIT or BROWSE modes.

It is necessary to close all files before exiting dBASE to the operating system. Always QUIT dBASE to return to the operating system to prevent possible loss of data or damage to open files that might not have been closed.

dBASE DEFAULT SETTINGS

There are commands that permit you to display information about the dBASE default settings and disk drive. The ability to view and change these settings and designations is available by using the SET command.

With SET you can view and change ON/OFF SET commands, function key assignments, default drive and search path, left margin, decimal places, index files, and format files.

Viewing dBASE Default Settings and Disk Drive Information

1. Type SET and press RETURN.

Changing a Default Setting

1. Type SET and press RETURN. Selected items (ON) and categories are highlighted.
2. Select a function group by using the left and right arrow keys.
3. Select a specific item from within a category by using the up and down arrow keys.
4. Press the space bar to change the value of the highlighted option.

STATUS OF CURRENT dBASE SESSION

For each open database file, Display Status shows the database filename, the current work area, index files that are open, the index key for each open index file, the current file search path, the left margin setting, function key assignments, the device setting (Screen or Print), and current settings for most ON/OFF SET commands.

Viewing Information about the Status of the Current Session of dBASE

1. Type DISPLAY STATUS and press RETURN.

Printing the Current Status of the dBASE Work Session

1. Type DISPLAY STATUS TO PRINT and press RETURN.

Creating Files

CREATING A DATABASE FILE

The database file has two parts: a file structure and records. The file structure is the list of fields that indicate the kinds of information found in the file. Records are the stored data.

To create a database file, first create the file structure and then enter data, record by record.

Creating a Database File Structure

Creating a database file structure in dBASE III is done by using screen menu options. The arrow keys (on the 2, 4, 6, and 8 numeric keys of the keyboard) move the cursor to any field. The field information required is highlighted. Type in the necessary information and press RETURN to move to the next field. To see other options displayed, press SPACE BAR until the option you want appears. Press RETURN to select that option and move to the next field. The cursor does not advance if the field is incompletely defined.

Instructions and/or error messages will appear at the bottom of the screen.

1. Type CREATE at the dot(.) prompt and press RETURN.
2. Type < filename> and press RETURN.

Example: NEWFILE < RETURN>

dBASE III displays the file structure menu of a record on the screen. The screen display also indicates the database file name and the number of characters available in the record.

3. Enter the < fieldname> and press RETURN.

The cursor is positioned on the screen display Char/text.

4. Press RETURN if the field type is a character type.

or

Enter the first character (C,N,L,D, or M) of the field type at the **field type** option.

or

Press SPACE BAR until your choice of field type appears.

5. Press RETURN to select field type and move to the next file structure menu option.

To directly select the field type, type the first letter of the field type. It is not necessary to press RETURN.

The cursor moves to the field width column.

6. Enter the width of your field and press RETURN.

In numeric fields, remember to count the decimal point as one of the number of places needed.

Note: dBASE III automatically enters the width of a DATE field as eight characters (mm/dd/yy).

7. dBASE III bypasses the decimal column for all field types except the numeric fields and positions the cursor at the field name of the next record.

For numeric fields, enter the number of decimal places to the right of the decimal point and press RETURN.

8. Repeat steps 3–7 until all fields are entered and the file structure is defined.

Ending Entry of Database File Structure and Remaining in dBASE

1. Press RETURN when cursor is positioned in a blank field or press CTRL

END(^END) to exit CREATE.

Typing any other key will continue data entry of fields.

2. A screen prompt will ask INPUT DATA RECORDS NOW? (Y/N). Type N. (A small letter n is also recognized).
3. The newly created file is saved, and you are returned to the dot prompt in dBASE III.

You have the option of typing **Y** for yes and entering data immediately.

It is prudent to review the structure of the newly created file before entering data. The file structure can be easily changed if no data has yet been entered.

Exiting dBASE and Returning to the Operating System

Warning: *Always* terminate a dBASE session with QUIT to prevent damage to open files and data loss.

1. Type QUIT and press RETURN.

All files in use are closed. The operating system prompt appears on screen.

CREATING MEMO FIELDS IN A DATABASE FILE

Memo fields are used to store text (up to 4000 characters).
  The memo field occupies only ten spaces of the database file, because the memo itself is stored in a separate disk file (.dbt).
  A rule of thumb: 50 characters or less is a character field; more than 50 characters should be a memo field.
  Memo fields are used to store Comments, Summaries, or other text.
  A maximum of 128 memo fields are allowed per record.
  Both the .dbf and the .dbt files must be copied whenever the database file is copied.

Creating a Memo Field in a File Structure

1. Type CREATE at the dot(.) prompt and press RETURN.
2. Type < database filename> and press RETURN when prompted on the screen.
3. Type **M** at the field type option or press SPACE BAR until MEMO field type appears.

4. Press RETURN to select field type and move to the next menu selection (DECIMAL).
5. Continue to select options from the CREATE menu and define the fields in the file structure.

Ending Entry of Memo Fields

1. Press RETURN when the cursor is positioned in a blank field or press CTRL END to exit CREATE.

   Typing any other key will continue data entry of fields.

2. A screen prompt will ask INPUT DATA NOW? (Y/N). Type N. (A small letter n is also recognized).
3. The newly created file is saved, and you are returned to the dot prompt in dBASE III.

Entering Data

ADDING DATA

Data can be entered into a database file by APPEND, INSERT, or BROWSE. New data are entered at the end of the file with APPEND or BROWSE. The file structure of one record is displayed on screen with APPEND. BROWSE displays up to 17 records and as many fields as the screen can contain. New data are inserted at the current record position with INSERT.

A file must be opened (USE) before data can be entered.

- Text enclosed in < > is determined by you.
- **Do not type the < > when typing your text.**

ADDING RECORDS TO A DATABASE FILE WITH APPEND

The APPEND command adds a new blank record to the end of the database file and permits data entry into this new blank record.

Full-screen editing is provided. The PgUp and PgDn keys move the cursor to the preceeding record or the next record. The arrow keys (on the 2,4,6 and 8 numeric keys) move the cursor down, left, up, and right within the fields of the record.

Adding Data with APPEND and No Index Files in Use

No index files are updated to include newly added data.

1. Type USE <database filename> and press RETURN if the data file is not in use.
2. Type APPEND and press RETURN.
3. Enter the data for the first record field.
4. Press RETURN.

   Information is entered by records, one field at a time. Each time you press RETURN, the cursor moves to a new field in the current record. If you are at the last field, pressing RETURN will display a new record.

Adding Additional New Records

5. Press CTRL and PgDn (^PgDn) after entering data in the last field to continue adding new records and data as needed.

Adding Data to a Database File with APPEND and Index Files in Use in the Current Work Area

All index files that are active during APPEND are updated to include newly added data.

1. Type USE <database filename> INDEX <index filename> and press RETURN if the data file is not in use.
2. Type APPEND and press RETURN.
3. Enter the data for the first record field.
4. Press RETURN.

   Information is entered by records, one field at a time. Each time you press RETURN, the cursor moves to a new field in the current record. If you are at the last field, pressing RETURN will display a new record.

5. Continue to enter data, one field at a time until all data are entered.

Moving to the Next Record

6. Press CTRL and PgDn (^PgDn). Do not enter any data in the blank field.

Adding a Blank Record to the End of a Database File

The blank record becomes the current record if you close the file after adding the blank record. The next time you open (USE) the file and go to the end of file (EOF), no data will be displayed, only the blank record.

The full-screen editing mode is *not* entered.

1. Type USE <database filename> and press RETURN if the data file is not in use.
2. Type APPEND BLANK and press RETURN.

ADDING RECORDS WITH BROWSE

The BROWSE command displays up to 17 records and as many fields as fit on the screen.

Full-screen editing is provided. See *Adding Records with APPEND*.

The current record is always displayed at the top of the screen when BROWSE is issued.

New records are added at the end of the database file.

Adding a New Record to a Database File with BROWSE

1. Type USE <database filename> and press RETURN if the data file is not in use.
2. Type BROWSE and press RETURN.
3. Type GO BOTTOM and press RETURN to move to the last record in the database file.
4. Press the down arrow (numeric key 2) to move beyond the last record and append a blank record.

If the current record was the last record in the database file, you may omit the GO BOTTOM command.

ADDING RECORDS WITH THE INSERT COMMAND

The INSERT command inserts one new record to the active database file at the current record location.

Full screen data entry is permitted with the INSERT command. See *Adding Records with APPEND*.

Inserting a New Record After the Current Record

1. Type USE <database filename> and press RETURN if the data file is not in use.

2. Type GO n and press RETURN. n is the record number after which a new record is inserted.
3. Type INSERT and press RETURN.

Inserting a New Record in a Database File before the Current Record

1. Type USE <database filename> and press RETURN if the data file is not in use.
2. Type GO n and press RETURN. n is the record number before which you wish to insert a new record.
3. Type INSERT BEFORE and press RETURN.

INSERTING BLANK RECORDS

With INSERT BLANK, a new record is inserted into the database file. Full-screen edit mode is *not* activated. Data may be entered later using BROWSE, EDIT, or CHANGE.

Inserting a Blank Record in a Database File at the Current Record

1. Type USE <database filename> and press RETURN if the data file is not in use.
2. Type GO n and press RETURN. n is the record number after which you wish to insert a new record.
3. Type INSERT BLANK and press RETURN.

Inserting a Blank Record in a Database File before the Current Record

1. Type USE <database filename> and press RETURN if the data file is not in use.
2. Type GO n and press RETURN. n is the record number before which you wish to insert a new record.
3. Type INSERT BLANK BEFORE and press RETURN.

ADDING DATA TO A MEMO FIELD

Data entered in a memo field are a text file and are entered using the dBASE text editor or a text editor of your choice.

Adding Data to a Memo Field with APPEND

1. Type USE <database filename> and press RETURN if the data file is not in use.
2. Type APPEND and press RETURN.
3. Press CTRL and PgDn(^PgDn) with the cursor positioned at MEMO field type.

MODIFY COMMAND is the dBASE text editor. The control keys used to APPEND data to a memo field are the same as for MODIFY COMMAND.

Adding Data to a Memo Field with BROWSE

Adding data to a memo field cannot be done with the BROWSE command.

Adding Data to a Memo Field with INSERT

1. Type USE <database filename> and press RETURN if the data file is not in use.
2. Position the cursor on the word MEMO.
3. Press CTRL and PgDn(^PgDn).
4. Add data to the memo field using the dBASE text editor or a text editor of your choice.

The control keys used to add data to a memo field are the same as the control keys used in MODIFY COMMAND.

Saving Files

SAVING A FILE STRUCTURE

Saving a Newly Created Database File Structure

1. Press RETURN when the cursor is positioned in a blank field (or after the 32nd field) to indicate that all fields have been entered.
2. A screen prompt will ask INPUT DATA NOW? (Y/N). Type N.
3. The newly created file is saved, and you are returned to the dot prompt in dBASE III.

   You have the option of typing Y for yes and entering data immediately.

   It is prudent to review the structure of the newly created file before entering data. The file structure can be changed easily if no data have yet been entered.

4. Type USE <data filename> and press RETURN.
5. Type DISPLAY STRUCTURE and press RETURN.

   The newly created file structure will be displayed on the screen, followed by the dot prompt ready for the next dBASE command.

6. Type QUIT to close the file and exit to the operating system.

SAVING DATA IN APPEND

Many texts, including the dBASE III manual, indicate the CONTROL key with the symbol ^. Directions to enter ^/ followed by a letter or other key indicate that you should press the CONTROL (CTRL) key followed by the letter or other key specified.

Saving All Data Entered and Exiting APPEND from the Current Record

1. Press CTRL and END (^END). All data additions are saved, and you are returned to the dot prompt of dBASE.

Saving All Data Entered and Exiting APPEND from a Blank Record

1. Press RETURN when the new record is displayed. You are returned to the dot prompt of dBASE. The file will not have a blank record as the last record.

Or

1. Press the CTRL and END keys. All data additions are saved, and you remain in dBASE. A blank record remains in the file and is indicated in the number of records in the file.

Saving All Data Entered Except That in the Current Record

1. Press ESC or CTRL and W (^W). You are returned to the dBASE prompt.

SAVING DATA IN INSERT

Saving Data Added with the INSERT Command

1. Press CTRL and END (^END). Data are inserted into the record and saved. You are returned to the dot prompt of dBASE.

Exiting INSERT without Saving Newly Added Data

1. Press ESC. No data are inserted into the record. You are returned to the dot prompt of dBASE.

SAVING DATA IN EDIT

Saving Changes in the Record and Advancing One Record

1. Press PgDn or CTRL and C (^C). The changes are saved. You remain in EDIT.

Saving Changes in the Record and Moving Back One Record

1. Press PgUp or CTRL and R (^R).

Saving All Changes Made in the File and Exiting EDIT

1. Press CTRL and END or CTRL and W (^W). You are returned to the dot prompt of dBASE.

Exiting EDIT without Saving Changes Made in the Current Record

1. Press ESC or CTRL and Q (^Q). All changes except those in the current record are saved. You are returned to the dot prompt of dBASE.

SAVING CHANGES IN BROWSE

Saving Changes Made in BROWSE and Advancing to the Next Window

1. Press PgDn or CTRL and C (^C).

Saving Changes Made in BROWSE and Moving Back One Window

1. Press PgUp or CTRL and R (^R).

Saving All Changes and Exiting BROWSE

1. Press CTRL and END or CTRL and W (^W). You are returned to the dot prompt of dBASE.

Exiting BROWSE without Saving the Current Entry

1. Press ESC or CTRL and Q (^Q). All changes except those in the current record are saved. You are returned to the dot prompt of dBASE.

Exiting a Memo Field and Saving Newly Added Data

1. Press END to save changes.

Exiting a Memo Field without Saving Newly Added Data

1. Press ESC.

Viewing Data

VIEWING OPTIONS

Viewing data in a database file requires that the database file be open, that the information to be viewed be specified, that a command to display or list the specified information be issued, and that the file be closed if no further work in the file is intended.

dBASE III provides the user with several options in viewing the records in a database file. The user views one record, all records, or some records. It is also possible to view just certain fields of one record, of all records, or of some records.

ADJUSTING THE POINTER

Moving about within a database file is done by use of a **pointer**, which keeps track of the records in the file. The pointer is not seen by the user. It is the means by which dBASE III internally locates the specified information stored in the file.

The **absolute** position is the position where the data are stored. Commands that adjust the pointer position according to the absolute position of the data as stored in the file include:

GO TOP: Positions the pointer at the first record.

GO BOTTOM: Positions the pointer at the last record.

n: Positions the pointer at the specified (n) record (ALTERNATE: GO n).

USE <filename>: Opens the file with the pointer at the first record.

APPEND: Positions the pointer at the end of file.

EDIT: Positions the pointer at the current record if the file is already in use; at the first record if the file has just been opened.

BROWSE: See EDIT.

Commands that adjust the pointer position relative to its last position include:

SKIP: Moves the pointer forward to the next record.

SKIP n: Moves the pointer forward n records from the current record position.

SKIP -n: Moves the pointer back n records from the current record position.

NEXT n: Moves the pointer through the next n records from the current position when used as a scope qualifier in a command.

VIEWING AN EXISTING DATABASE FILE

The command to open a database file (USE) does not display the records on screen. Commands to display data on the screen will produce different viewing results depending upon the scope of the command and on whether or not the database file is already in use.

If the file is NOT already open, typing USE and pressing RETURN positions the cursor at the first record of the database to begin viewing.

If the file is already in USE, the record displayed is the current record at the pointer position or relative to the current record position, depending upon the command issued.

VIEWING RECORDS OF A DATABASE FILE

The database file must be opened (USE) before any data stored in the records of the file can be found and displayed.

Records can be viewed with a LIST command, which scrolls (moves the records continuously up and off the screen), or with DISPLAY.

LIST without any scope qualifiers displays all records on the screen. DISPLAY without scope qualifiers shows only the current record of a file in USE.

Viewing All Records with Screen Scrolling

1. Type USE <database filename> and press RETURN if the data file is not in use.
2. Type LIST and press RETURN.
3. Type CTRL and S (^S) to stop scrolling of records.
4. Type CTRL and S (^S) to restart scrolling of records.

   The LIST command displays the entire data file, scrolling the records until the end of the file is reached.

Viewing All Records One Screen at a Time

1. Type USE <database filename> and press RETURN if the data file is not in use.
2. Type DISPLAY ALL and press RETURN.

   The DISPLAY command displays 15 records at a time on the screen.

3. Press SPACE BAR to continue viewing the data file.

Viewing the First Record

1. Type USE <database filename> and press RETURN if the data file is not in use.
2. Type DISPLAY and press RETURN.

Viewing the Last Record

1. Type USE <database filename> and press RETURN if the data file is not in use.
2. Type GO BOTTOM and press RETURN.
3. Type DISPLAY and press RETURN.

Viewing a Specific Record

1. Type USE <database filename> and press RETURN if the data file is not in use.
2. Type DISPLAY RECORD <n> and press RETURN. You must enter the record number for n.

   or

2. Type GOTO RECORD n and press RETURN.
3. Type DISPLAY and press RETURN to view the record.

Viewing Records by a Specific Date

dBASE III does not store dates the way you enter them.

Dates are entered in the MM/DD/YY form and are stored in the YYYYMMDD form. To match a date contained in the data file, you must convert the form using the DTOC function (date to character).

Failure to convert the date form results in an error message "Data Type Mismatch."

In dBASE III, dates and Zipcodes are usually defined as character data and should be enclosed in quotes when locating records with matching data.

1. Type USE <database filename> and press RETURN if the data file is not in use.
2. Type DISPLAY ALL FOR DTOC(Date) = 'date to be matched in MM/DD/YY form' and press RETURN.

VIEWING DATA USING LOGICAL OPERATORS .AND., .OR., .NOT.

The **logical operator** states how two items should be related: Both stated conditions must be true (.AND.); only one of two stated conditions must be true (.OR.); or only items for which the condition is false are to be selected.

The period (.) *must* be typed before and after .AND., .OR., and .NOT..

- Character data to be matched must be enclosed in quotes. Numeric data to be matched are not enclosed in quotes.

Commands that use logical operators sometimes exceed the length of one line. A semicolon at the end of the first command line tells dBASE that there is more to come. Commands that are longer than one line must include a semicolon at the end of the line.

Viewing Records Using .AND.

1. Type USE <database filename> and press RETURN if the data file is not in use.
2. Type DISPLAY ALL FOR <fieldname 1> = 'data to be matched' .AND. <fieldname 2> = 'data to be matched' and press RETURN.

   Example: DISPLAY ALL FOR lastname = 'Smith' .AND. zipcode = '60120'. The record to be displayed must have the same first and second fieldnames as specified in the command.

Viewing Records Using .OR.

1. Type USE <database filename> and press RETURN if the data file is not in use.

2. Type DISPLAY ALL FOR <fieldname 1> = 'data to be matched' .OR. <fieldname 2> = 'data to be matched' and press RETURN.

   Example: DISPLAY ALL FOR lastname = 'Smith .OR. zipcode = '60120'
   The record must match either the first or the second condition.

Viewing Records Using .NOT.

1. Type USE <database filename> and press RETURN if the data file is not in use.
2. Type DISPLAY ALL FOR .NOT. <fieldname> = 'data to be matched' and press RETURN.

   Example: DISPLAY ALL FOR .NOT. lastname = 'Smith'

VIEWING DATA USING RELATIONAL OPERATORS <, >, =, <>

<> or # are the symbols for not equal on the computer. Type the <> without any space between them.

Viewing Records That Are Greater Than a Specified Value

1. Type USE <database filename> and press RETURN if the data file is not in use.
2. Type DISPLAY ALL FOR <fieldname> > <numeric value> and press RETURN.

Viewing Records That Are Greater Than or Equal to a Specified Value

1. Type USE <database filename> and press RETURN if the data file is not in use.
2. Type DISPLAY ALL FOR <fieldname> >= <numeric value> and press RETURN.

Viewing Records That Are Less Than a Specified Value

1. Type USE <database filename> and press RETURN if the data file is not in use.
2. Type DISPLAY ALL FOR <fieldname> < <numeric value> and press RETURN.

Viewing Records That Are Less Than or Equal to a Specified Value

1. Type USE <database filename> and press RETURN if the data file is not in use.
2. Type DISPLAY ALL FOR <fieldname> <= <numeric value> and press RETURN.

Viewing Records That Are Not Equal to a Specified Numeric Value

1. Type USE <database filename> and press RETURN if the data file is not in use.
2. Type DISPLAY ALL FOR <fieldname> <> <numeric value> and press RETURN.

Viewing Records That Are Not Equal to a Specified Character Value

1. Type USE <database filename> and press RETURN if the data file is not in use.
2. Type DISPLAY ALL FOR <fieldname> <> 'character value' and press RETURN.

VIEWING RECORDS WITH OR WITHOUT RECORD NUMBERS

Records are displayed with the record number and all fields listed across the screen followed by the individual records in a row and column format. Records are read horizontally across the screen under the field headings for each column.
    The **record number** is a number assigned by dBASE III to each record as a unique identifier for locating, retrieving, sorting, and displaying each record.

Viewing All Records with No Record Numbers Displayed

1. Type USE <database filename> and press RETURN if the data file is not in use.
2. Type DISPLAY ALL OFF and press RETURN.

Viewing Specific Fields with Record Numbers

1. Type USE <database filename> and press RETURN if the data file is not in use.
2. Type DISPLAY ALL <fieldname 1, fieldname 2> and press RETURN.

   Note: The fields will be displayed in the order in which they are listed in the command.

Viewing Specific Fields without Record Numbers

1. Type USE <database filename> and press RETURN if the data file is not in use.
2. Type LIST OFF <fieldname 1, fieldname 2> and press RETURN.

   Note: The fields will be displayed in the order in which they are listed in the command.

Viewing Only Records for Which the Command Expression Is True

1. Type USE <database filename> and press RETURN if the data file is not in use.
2. Type DISPLAY ALL FOR <fieldname> = 'data to be matched' and press RETURN.

   Example: DISPLAY ALL FOR ZIPCODE = '99999'.

   Note: The record number(s) will be displayed on screen for which the condition is true.

Character data to be matched must be enclosed in quotes. Numeric data to be matched are not enclosed in quotes.

VIEWING RECORDS IN A DATABASE FILE THAT IS ALREADY IN USE

Viewing records in a database file that is already in use sometimes has a command sequence that consists of more than the omission of the first command: Type USE <database filename> and press RETURN.

Viewing the First Record

1. Type GO TOP and press RETURN.
2. Type DISPLAY and press RETURN.

Viewing a Record Following the Last One Displayed in the Database File

1. Type DISPLAY and press RETURN.
2. Type SKIP <n> and press RETURN.
3. Type DISPLAY and press RETURN.

Viewing a Record That Precedes the Last One Displayed in the Database File

1. Type DISPLAY and press RETURN.
2. Type SKIP -n and press RETURN.
3. Type DISPLAY and press RETURN.

Changing Data

COMMANDS THAT CHANGE DATA

Data can be changed by overwriting existing text, inserting text, or replacing text. The dBASE III commands that permit data to be changed using full-screen editing include EDIT and BROWSE. New data are substituted for existing data with the REPLACE command.

EDIT displays one record at a time. BROWSE displays up to 17 records at a time.

Both EDIT and BROWSE use full-screen key operations.

MOVING THE CURSOR USING EDIT OR BROWSE

In the EDIT or BROWSE mode there are the following full-screen commands that move the cursor around from field to field of one record and from record to record.

Moving the Cursor Down One Field

1. Press the down arrow (numeric key 2) or CTRL and X (^X).

Moving the Cursor Back to the Previous Field

1. Press the up arrow (numeric key 8) or CTRL and E (^E).

Moving the Cursor to the Right One Character

1. Press the right arrow (numeric key 6) or CTRL and D (^D).

Moving the Cursor to the Left One Character

1. Press the left arrow (numeric key 4) or CTRL and S (^S).

Moving One Word to the Right

1. Press END or CTRL and F (^F).

Moving One Word to the Left

1. Press HOME or CTRL and A (^A).

INSERTING DATA

Inserting a New Line or Field Definition

1. Press CTRL and N (^N).

DELETING CHARACTERS

Deleting the Character at the Cursor

1. Press DEL or CTRL and G (^G).

Deleting the Character to the Left of the Cursor

1. Press the backspace arrow (top key row) or type RUB.

Deleting One Word to the Right of the Cursor Position

1. Press CTRL and T (^T).

Deleting Data to the End of the Field

1. Press CTRL and Y (^Y).

MARKING AND UNMARKING RECORDS FOR DELETION

Marking a Record for Deletion

1. Press CTRL and U (^U). The word "DELETED" appears at the top of your screen.

Removing the Deletion Mark from a Record

1. Press CTRL and U (^U) a second time. The word "DELETED" is removed from the screen, and the record is no longer marked for deletion.

EDITING DATA

The EDIT mode applies only to the current record displayed unless the scope (ALL, NEXT n, RECORD n) is stated in the command.

In the EDIT mode, characters at the cursor position are overwritten.

Changing Data in a Database Record Using the EDIT Command

1. Type USE <database filename> and press RETURN if the data file is not in use.
2. Type EDIT and press RETURN.

Changing from EDIT (Overwrite Mode) to INSERT (Insert Mode)

In the INSERT mode, a character is inserted before the cursor. The INSERT mode can be toggled on or off when in the EDIT mode.

1. Press INS or CTRL and V (^V). The first CTRL V inserts data into the field before the cursor. The second CTRL V turns the INSERT mode off and resumes overwriting of existing data in the field at the cursor.

BROWSING A DATABASE FILE

The BROWSE mode has the same full screen commands as the EDIT mode. However, BROWSE displays up to 17 records and as many fields as your screen display permits at one time.

The current record is displayed at the top of the screen when the BROWSE command is issued.

Changing Data Using the BROWSE Command

1. Press USE <database filename> and press RETURN if the data file is not in use.
2. Type BROWSE and press RETURN.

Moving the Display Window One Field to the Right

1. Press CTRL and the right arrow (numeric key 6) or CTRL and B (^B).

Moving the Display Window One Field to the Left

1. Press CTRL and the left arrow (numeric key 4) or CTRL and Z (^Z).

Moving the Display Window Down

1. Press PgDn.

Moving the Display Window Up

1. Press PgUp.

Rearranging Data

INDEX AND SORT COMPARISONS

Data can be rearranged by sorting the records or by indexing the records. The SORT command reorders records of the database in use and changes the record numbers in the sorted file.

The INDEX command sets up a new database file (index file) that specifies the order in which records should be listed. The order of records and the record numbers are unchanged by the INDEX command.

Sorting requires more storage space and usually takes more time than indexing a database file.

Indexed files that are in use with the database file are automatically updated whenever changes are made to the database file. Database files must be resorted whenever changes are made to the file.

It is easier to SORT fields of different types (character and numeric) than it is to INDEX on mixed field types.

Information arranged from most current to earliest should be sorted by date.

Both INDEX and SORT rearrange data in an ascending order by default. It is possible to INDEX and to SORT in descending order as well.

Records marked for deletion are indexed. If SET DELETED is OFF, records marked for deletion are sorted.

Both the SORT and INDEX commands leave the original database file intact with the records in the order in which they were entered or edited.

SORTING FILES

The SORT command creates and saves a new sorted file that contains all of the data of the original file. The sorted file has a .dbf extension. The original database file still exists unchanged by the SORT command.

The SORT command rearranges the records of the active (in current USE) database file alphabetically, by date, or numerically, based on the specified key field expression.

Any character, numeric, or date field can be used as the key field for the SORT command. Memo fields or logical fields cannot be used as key fields with the SORT command.

Substrings and complex expresions cannot be used as key expressions with the SORT command. Use INDEX in these instances.

A file cannot be sorted to itself or to any other file in use.

The sorted file must be in USE to view results of a SORT.

The SORT command should be used instead of the INDEX command when:

- the file is never, or rarely going to be changed;
- needed information is to be printed sequentially;
- information is needed in reverse alphabetical order;
- dates are needed in order from latest to earliest;
- different alphabetical keys are in different orders.

New or revised data in the database file will not be updated in a sorted file. Each time new data or revisions are entered in the original database file, the database file must be resorted.

Records marked for deletion are *not* sorted unless SET DELETED is turned OFF.

SORT rearranges the records in ascending order by default.

Caution: Never SORT a file directly without first making a copy of the file.

Protect the original data, particularly in large files, by first making a copy of the file and then sorting the copy to a sorted file name that indicates how the file was sorted.

Since SORT duplicates the size of the original file, check to see that you have sufficient disk space for the copy *before* beginning a SORT.

Sorting a File

1. Type USE <database filename> and press RETURN if the data file is not already in use.
2. Type SORT ON <key field> TO <sorted filename> and press RETURN.

   If SET DELETED command is OFF, deleted records (those marked for deletion and not removed by a PACK command) will be sorted and appear in the newly sorted file marked for deletion as in the original file.

   If the SET DELETED command is ON, deleted records will not be sorted and included in the new sorted file.
3. Type USE <sorted filename> and press RETURN.
4. Type DISPLAY ALL and press RETURN to view the results of the SORT.

Sorting a Database File without Differentiating Upper or Lower Case

/C is used when upper and lower case differentiation is to be ignored.

1. Type USE <database filename> and press RETURN if the data file is not already in use.
2. Type SORT ON <data filename/C> TO <sorted filename> and press RETURN.
3. Type USE <sorted filename> and press RETURN.
4. Type DISPLAY ALL and press RETURN to view the results of the SORT.

Sorting a Database File on Descending Order

D and A are used to indicate descending or ascending sorts.

1. Type USE <database filename> and type RETURN if the data file is not already in use.
2. Type SORT ON <fieldname/D> TO <sorted filename> and press RETURN.
3. Type USE <sorted filename> and press RETURN.
4. Type DISPLAY ALL and press RETURN to view the results of the SORT.

Sorting on a Date Field (Latest to Earliest)

D indicates a descending order sort.

1. Type USE <database filename> and press RETURN if the data file is not already in use.
2. Type SORT ON DATE/D TO SORTDOWN and press RETURN.
3. Type USE SORTDOWN and press RETURN.
4. Type DISPLAY ALL and press RETURN to view the results of the SORT.

Sorting on More Than One Field of the Same Type

The most important field should be sorted first.

1. Type SORT ON <1st fieldname, 2nd fieldname> TO <sorted filename> and press RETURN.

INDEXING FILES

The INDEX command creates a new index file with an .ndx extension that contains only a list of the order the records would be in if the file were sorted. The INDEX file does not contain all of the information contained in the original database file or in a sorted file.

The index file saves time and disk space and, for most purposes, will accomplish the same things as a sorted file. It is possible to have a maximum of seven index files for a single database file open at the same time.

Index files can be ordered in a logical sequence (alphabetical, chronological, or numerical) based on a character, numeric, or date key field or fields. Memo and logical fields cannot be indexed.

The key field or expression specifies the desired order of the index file and can be any item contained in the record (such as Lastname, State, Zipcode, Date, etc).

The INDEX command rearranges the data in ascending order by default on a key field or expression.

A maximum of 100 characters is permitted in the key expression.

Indexing on a Character Field Type

1. Type USE <database filename> and press RETURN if the data file is not in use.
2. Type INDEX ON <key field expression> TO <index filename> and press RETURN.

   Example: INDEX ON lname TO lastname <RETURN>

3. Type DISPLAY ALL and press RETURN to view the results of the INDEX command.

Indexing on Numeric Fields

1. Type USE <database filename> and press RETURN if the data file is not already in use.
2. Type INDEX ON <key field expression> TO <index filename> and press RETURN.
3. Type DISPLAY ALL and press RETURN to view the results of the INDEX command.

Indexing on a Date Field (Earliest to Latest)

Dates are entered and displayed in mm/dd/yy format.

1. Type USE <database filename> and press RETURN if the data file is not already in use.
2. Type INDEX ON DATE TO DATEINDX and press RETURN.
3. Type DISPLAY ALL and press RETURN to view the results of the INDEX command.

Indexing on a Date Field (Latest to Earliest)

The easiest way to accomplish this is to use the SORT command. See *SORTING FILES: Sorting on the date field (latest to earliest)*.

Indexing on More Than One Field of the Same Type

1. Type USE <database filename> and press RETURN if the data file is not already in use.
2. Type INDEX ON <field 1 + field 2 + field 3> TO <index filename> and press RETURN.
3. Type DISPLAY ALL and press RETURN to view results of INDEX command.

Note: The INDEX command used on more than one field rearranges the data in the order in which the fields are listed.

Indexing on Two Fields That Are Not of the Same Type

The INDEX command cannot index on two fields that are of different types such as a character field and a numeric field. To index fields of different data types, first convert all fields to the same type.

Use the function STR(). This function converts a numeric value into a character value.

45

1. Type USE <database filename> and press RETURN if the data file is not in use.
2. Type INDEX ON <character field> + STR(numeric fieldname, width of field, number of decimal places) TO <index filename> and press RETURN.

    Example: INDEX ON custno + STR(amount,10,2) TO <duefrom>

3. Type DISPLAY ALL and press RETURN to view the results of the INDEX command.

INDEXING IN DESCENDING ORDER

When the Key Field Is a Character Type

Use the special function ASC(). This function uses a numeric value equal to the ASCII value of the first character in the field on which the file is to be indexed.

This numeric value may be multiplied by (-1) to create a descending order.

1. Type USE <database filename> and press RETURN if the data file is not in use.
2. Type INDEX ON <-fieldname>*-1 TO <index filename> and press RETURN.
3. Type DISPLAY ALL and press RETURN to view the results of the INDEX command.

When the Key Field Is Numeric

Use the negative value of the numeric field.

1. Type USE <database filename> and press RETURN if the data file is not in use.
2. Type INDEX ON <-numeric field>*-1 TO <index filename> and press RETURN.
3. Type DISPLAY ALL and press RETURN to view the results of the INDEX command.

Locating Data

LOCATING INFORMATION

Locating information in a database file is done by searching the database file or by searching an indexed file. It is possible to locate information by record, by field, or by a string of characters (characters enclosed in quotation marks) found in a particular field or record.

Finding information in an INDEX file requires the use of the FIND and SEEK commands. These commands work only on an indexed file and are used with the key field on which the file was indexed.

Locating information in any database file, including indexed files, can be found with the LOCATE and CONTINUE commands.

The LOCATE command is slower than the FIND command. On a large database file it is quicker to INDEX the file and locate information with the FIND command.

FINDING INFORMATION USING LOCATE

Information can be found by using fields other than the indexed fields with the LOCATE command. The LOCATE command also works with indexed fields.

LOCATE searches the file sequentially. Only the first record containing the data to be found is located in the file.

The CONTINUE command followed by the DISPLAY command displays the other records that contain the data looked for. Repeat these two commands to move through the database file.

Locating Records Based on the First Data Character

1. Type USE < database filename > and press RETURN if the data file is not in use.
2. Type LOCATE FOR < fieldname > = 'letter to be found' and press RETURN.

   Example: LOCATE FOR lastname = 'M'

3. Type DISPLAY and press RETURN.

Locating Records for a Specified Field .AND. Date

1. Type USE < database filename > and press RETURN if the data file is not in use.
2. Type LOCATE FOR < fieldname > = 'letter to be found' .AND. DTOC(DATE) = 'date to be found' and press RETURN.

   Example: LOCATE FOR item_no = 'CX10267'.AND. DTOC(DATE) = '09/25/85'

3. Type DISPLAY and press RETURN.

Locating Records for a Specified Field .OR. Date

1. Type USE < database filename > and press RETURN if the data file is not in use.
2. Type LOCATE FOR < fieldname > = ' < letter to be found > '.OR. DTOC(DATE) = ' < date to be found > ' and press RETURN.

   Example: LOCATE FOR item_no = 'CX10267'.OR. DTOC(DATE) = '09/25/85'

3. Type DISPLAY and press RETURN.

Locating Specific Data Contained in Records in the File

1. Type USE < database filename > and press RETURN if the data file is not in use.
2. Type LOCATE FOR < fieldname > = 'data to be found' and press RETURN.

   Example: LOCATE FOR lastname = 'Smith'
3. Type DISPLAY and press RETURN.

FINDING INFORMATION IN AN INDEXED FILE

There are two commands that quickly locate information in an indexed file: FIND and SEEK.

The FIND command searches the indexed file named in the command. This command is used with the key field or expression of an indexed file and locates only the first record in the file that matches the search conditions.

Only character string data can be located with FIND.

Any valid dBASE III expression can be found with the SEEK command, including those not located with the FIND command, provided that the data looked for match the INDEX key.

LOCATING INFORMATION USING FIND

The FIND command does not work with date fields, numeric data, or any dBASE functions such as DTOC (date to character conversion) and STR (numeric to character conversion).

The first character or characters in the key field must be specified for the FIND command to work.

Finding Records Based on the First Field Character

1. Type USE < database filename > and press RETURN if the data file is not in use.
2. Type INDEX ON < key fieldname > TO < index file name > and press RETURN.
3. Type FIND < first alphabetical character of data to be found > and press RETURN.

   Example: FIND M
4. Type DISPLAY and press RETURN.

Finding a Record Using an Indexed File

1. Type USE < database filename > INDEX < index filename > and press RETURN.
2. Type FIND < data to be matched > and press RETURN.
3. Type DISPLAY and press RETURN.

Note: An error message indicates that you do not have an indexed file for the field that contains the data you are looking for. Type INDEX ON < fieldname > TO < index filename > and press RETURN. Try the FIND again.

Finding a Record Using a Different Index File

1. Type USE < database filename > and press RETURN if the data file is not in use.
2. Type SET INDEX TO < different index filename > and press RETURN.
3. Type FIND < data to be matched > and press RETURN.
4. Type DISPLAY and press RETURN.

Finding Several Records

The FIND command locates only the first record in the file that matches the data being looked for. The cursor is positioned at the top of the file when FIND is issued.

The command to continue looking for more records after the first that match the search conditions is LIST WHILE. dBASE will continue to find and display records that match the search conditions until the entire file is searched.

For large databases, this command is preferable to repeating the three-step sequence DISPLAY, press RETURN, press PgDn to find all records in the file that match the specified conditions.

1. Type USE < database filename > INDEX < index filename > and press RETURN.
2. Type FIND < data to be matched > and press RETURN.
3. Type LIST WHILE < key fieldname > = ' < data to be matched > ' and press RETURN.

    Example: LIST WHILE lastname = 'Smith'
4. Press PgDn .
5. Type DISPLAY and press RETURN.

Finding Records Using a Combined Index of More Than One Field

The FIND command looks for data based on the total number of character spaces. Field data that contain fewer characters than the length of the field include blank spaces that you might not remember to enter when issuing the FIND command. Using TRIM with the first field solves the problem of matching total length correctly by removing any blank spaces in the first field.

1. Type USE < database filename > and press RETURN if the data file is not in use.
2. Type INDEX ON TRIM (< fieldname 1 >) + < fieldname 2 > TO < index filename > and press RETURN.

    Example: INDEX ON TRIM (dept) + item TO inventory

3. Type FIND < data to be matched > and press RETURN.
4. Type DISPLAY and press RETURN.

LOCATING INFORMATION USING SEEK

Numeric information can be found by using the SEEK command. This command is also used when information based on dates is needed.

Finding Data Indexed on a Date Field

1. Type USE < database filename > INDEX < date index filename > and press RETURN.
2. Type SEEK CTOD(' < date to be found > ') and press RETURN.
3. Type DISPLAY and press RETURN.

Deleting Data

REMOVING RECORDS

Removing records from a database file is a two-step process. Specific records are marked for deletion with the DELETE command. To permanently remove data from a database file requires a second command, PACK.

Records marked for deletion are indicated by an * when the file is viewed by using DISPLAY or LIST.

In full screen modes (EDIT or BROWSE), records marked for deletion are indicated by *DEL* on the status line.

Records marked for deletion can be reinstated in the database file by using the RECALL command.

The INDEX and REINDEX commands always include all records, including those marked for deletion.

If SET DELETED ON is used, the SORT command will *not* sort records marked for deletion, and the marked records will *not* be copied by using the COPY command.

All records marked for deletion will be included in a SORT or COPY command if SET DELETED OFF is used.

MARKING RECORDS FOR DELETION

Marking records for deletion does not remove the records from the database file. They can still be viewed, indexed, copied, and sorted.

Marking a Record for Deletion

1. Type USE <database filename> and press RETURN if the data file is not in use.
2. Type GOTO n and press RETURN.
3. Type DELETE and press RETURN.

   When the record is DISPLAYed, an asterisk preceeds the record data.

Marking Specified Records for Deletion by Field

1. Type USE <database filename> and press RETURN if the data file is not in use.
2. Type DELETE ALL FOR <fieldname> = 'data to be matched' and press RETURN.

   Note: Character data and dates need to be included in quotes. Numeric data to be matched are not enclosed in quotes.

Marking Specified Records for Deletion by Date

1. Type USE <database filename> and press RETURN if the data file is not in use.
2. Type DELETE ALL FOR DTOC(DATE) = 'date to be matched' and press RETURN.

   Note: Character data and dates need to be included in quotes. Numeric data to be matched are not enclosed in quotes.

Marking the Next Record(s) after the Current Record for Deletion

1. Type USE <database filename> and press RETURN if the data file is not in use.
2. Type DELETE NEXT n and press RETURN.

UNMARKING RECORDS PREVIOUSLY MARKED FOR DELETION

Records marked for deletion can be unmarked prior to a PACK command.

Unmarking a Record for Deletion in a Database File

1. Type USE <database filename> and press RETURN if the data file is not in use.
2. Type RECALL and press RETURN.

   RECALL reinstates only the current record.

   The RECALL command does *not* reinstate records that were previously removed from the database file with PACK or ZAP commands.

Unmarking All Records Marked for Deletion

1. Type USE <database filename> and press RETURN if the data file is not in use.
2. Type RECALL ALL and press RETURN.

   If SET DELETED is ON, RECALL ALL has no effect. Records must be recalled individually.

Unmarking Only the First Record Marked for Deletion

1. Type USE <database filename> and press RETURN if the data file is not in use.
2. Type RECALL and press RETURN.

Unmarking Specified Records Marked for Deletion

1. Type USE <database filename> and press RETURN if the data file is not in use.
2. Type RECALL ALL FOR <fieldname> = 'data to be matched' and press RETURN.

   Note: Character data and dates need to be included in quotes. Numeric data to be matched are not enclosed in quotes.

Unmarking Records Specified by Date Marked for Deletion

1. Type USE <database filename> and press RETURN if the data file is not in use.
2. Type RECALL ALL FOR DTOC(DATE) = 'date to be matched' and press RETURN.

   Note: Character data and dates need to be included in quotes. Numeric data to be matched are not enclosed in quotes.

REMOVING RECORDS MARKED FOR DELETION

Records can be removed from a database file selectively by using the PACK command.
   The PACK command removes only records that were previously marked for deletion. All open index files are automatically reindexed.

Removing All Records Previously Marked for Deletion

1. Type USE <database filename> and press RETURN if the data file is not in use.
2. Type DISPLAY ALL and press RETURN to verify that all records marked for deletion are to be removed from the database file.

   Warning: The following command erases the records from the file permanently. Once packed, records are gone.
3. Type PACK and press RETURN.

Removing a Specified Record That Has Previously Been Marked for Deletion

Single records may be marked for removal, but PACK removes all marked records, not just a specified record.
   There is no command to remove a single record from a file unless that is the only record marked for deletion and a PACK command is issued.

REMOVING ALL RECORDS FROM A DATABASE FILE

All records can be removed with a single command, ZAP. ZAP removes all records, marked and unmarked, from the file. If SET SAFETY is ON, you will be prompted to confirm the command to remove all records (Y/N). Type Y to remove all records. Any open index files of the database file in use are automatically removed along with the records in the database file.

All records can also be removed with a a two-step procedure using PACK.

Both ZAP and PACK remove records permanently, but ZAP is faster when all records are to be erased.

Removing All Records from a Database File Using ZAP

Warning: Look at the contents of a file before issuing the ZAP command. All records are permanently erased from the file.

1. Type USE <database filename> and press RETURN if the data file is not in use.
2. Type ZAP and press RETURN.

Removing All Records Using PACK

It is possible to remove all records by marking *all* records with the command DELETE ALL before issuing the PACK command.

1. Type USE <database filename> and press RETURN if the data file is not in use.
2. Type DELETE ALL and press RETURN.
3. Type PACK and press RETURN.

REMOVING FILES

A file, including all records, can be removed from a directory while in dBASE or at the operating system level.

The ERASE command in dBASE is like the ERASE command of DOS with the exception that in dBASE files are removed one at a time, by naming the file with its file extension. dBASE does not permit the use of *.*.

Any memo field files with .dbf extensions must be deleted separately. The memo file is not removed when the database file is erased.

Open files cannot be deleted while in dBASE.

In dBASE, DELETE FILE is the same as ERASE.

Removing a File

1. Type ERASE <filename.extension> and press RETURN.

DELETING DATA WHILE IN EDIT OR BROWSE MODE

While in the EDIT or BROWSE mode, it is possible to mark records for deletion, remove characters and/or words from the fields of a record, and unmark records that were previously marked for deletion.

Marking a Record for Deletion

1. Press CTRL and U (*cfex*U).

   The word "DELETED" appears at the top of your screen.

Removing the Deletion Mark from a Record

1. Press CTRL and U (^U) a second time.

   The word "DELETED" is removed from the screen, and the record is no longer marked for deletion.

Removing Records Marked for Deletion and No Active Index Files

1. Type PACK and press RETURN.

   Index files that are not in use in the current work area are not packed.

Deleting Information in a Field While in EDIT or BROWSE

1. Type USE <database filename> and press RETURN if the data file is not in use.
2. Type EDIT and press RETURN.

Deleting the Character at the Cursor

1. Press DEL or CTRL and G (^G).

Deleting the Character to the Left of the Cursor

1. Press the backspace arrow (top key row) or type RUB.

Deleting One Word to the Right of the Cursor Position

1. Press CTRL and T (^T).

Deleting Data to the End of the Field

1. Press CTRL and Y (^Y).

Global File Changes

USING GLOBAL FILE COMMANDS

Certain commands affect all or large numbers of records in the database file. Once the command has been issued, the change is permanent and cannot be undone. Commands that could destroy or permanently change large numbers of records include REPLACE, PACK, ZAP, CHANGE, and MODIFY STRUCTURE.

Before you issue any of these commands, the SET SAFETY should be ON. With SET SAFETY ON, dBASE provides an opportunity to cancel the command before any permanent change is made.

REPLACING RECORDS IN A DATABASE FILE

The REPLACE command changes the content of only the current record of the database file unless a scope qualifier is included with the command.

The field data being replaced must be of the same type as the replacement data.

The WITH expression (replacement data) length cannot exceed the field width in a numeric field.

The record pointer in the database file remains unchanged with the REPLACE command. No replacements are made if the pointer is at the end of file (EOF).

Replacing One Field in All Records of the Database File

1. Type USE <database filename > and press RETURN if the data file is not in use.
2. Type REPLACE ALL <fieldname > WITH ' <data replacement >' and press RETURN.
3. Type DISPLAY ALL and press RETURN to view replacements made.

Replacing One Field in One Record in a Database File

1. Type USE <database filename > and press RETURN if the data file is not in use.
2. Type REPLACE <fieldname > WITH ' <data replacement >' and press RETURN.
3. Type DISPLAY ALL and press RETURN to view replacements made.

Replacing One Field in Specified Records in a Database File

1. Type USE <database filename > and press RETURN if the data file is not in use.
2. Type REPLACE NEXT n <fieldname > WITH ' <data replacement >' and press RETURN.
3. Type DISPLAY ALL and press RETURN to view replacements made.

Replacing the Date Field for One Record in the Database File

1. Type USE <database filename > and press RETURN if the data file is not in use.

    To replace the date, the CTOD (character to date) function is used to convert character string dates as input to the form stored by dBASE III.

2. Type REPLACE DATE WITH CTOD ('<mm/dd/yy >') and press RETURN.

    Example: REPLACE DATE WITH CTOD ('06/17/87') and press RETURN.

3. Type DISPLAY ALL and press RETURN to view replacements made.

Replacing Selected Records for a Given Field of the Database File

1. Type USE <database filename> and press RETURN if the data file is not in use.
2. Type REPLACE <fieldname> WITH 'data replacement' FOR <fieldname> = 'data to be replaced' and press RETURN.

   Example: REPLACE Item_No WITH 'B10459' FOR Item_No = 'B102X' and press RETURN.

3. Type DISPLAY ALL and press RETURN to view replacements.

Replacing the Value of a Selected Record for a Given Field

1. Type USE <database filename> and press RETURN if the data file is not in use.
2. Type REPLACE ALL <fieldname> WITH *.5 <field name> FOR <fieldname> = 'data to be replaced' and press RETURN.

   Note: The * indicates multiplication.

   Example: REPLACE ALL Item_No WITH *.5Item_No FOR Item_No = 'B102X' and press RETURN.

3. Type DISPLAY ALL and press RETURN to view replacements made.

CHANGING SPECIFIED FIELDS AND RECORDS

CHANGE replaces data in selected fields of specified records by editing the named field in all records. PgDn and PgUp move the cursor forward or backward one record in the file. The arrow keys move the cursor about within the record.

The CHANGE command positions the cursor at the first record of the file unless a scope qualifier is included with the command.

Editing Specified Fields and Records

1. Type USE <database filename> and press RETURN if the data file is not in use.
2. Type CHANGE FIELDS <field 1, field 2, field 3> and press RETURN.

   Example: CHANGE FIELDS item_no, item_cost, quantity

UPDATING INDEX FILES

All active (those in use) index files are automatically updated whenever a change is made to the database file for those index files. Many times, not all index files are currently in use when the database file is in USE. Index files that are not in use will not be updated. You need to keep note of which index files are in use when the database file is changed and update index files accordingly.

Appended records will be automatically added to the open index files in correct order.

Opening Index Files before Changing the Database File

1. Type USE <database filename > and press RETURN if the database file is not currently in use.
2. Type SET INDEX TO <index key field 1, index key field 2>,

    The command SET INDEX TO opens the named index files. When changes are made to the database file, this command will update all index files that are in use with the current active database file.

Updating an Index File When Data Are Replaced in One Field

1. Type USE <database filename > INDEX <key field 1 > and press RETURN
2. Type REPLACE ALL <fieldname > WITH <data replacement > and press RETURN.

    Example: REPLACE ALL item_cost WITH item_cost*1.3

3. Type DISPLAY ALL and press RETURN to view replacements made.

    Do not make multiple replacements on an indexed field.

Removing All Records Marked for Deletion in a Database File

1. Type USE <database filename > and press RETURN if the data file is not in use.
2. Type PACK and press RETURN.

    If SET SAFETY is ON, a screen prompt will ask if you really want to do this (Y/N). Press Y to proceed.

Removing All Records from the Active Database File (including those NOT marked for deletion)

1. Type USE <database filename> and press RETURN if the data file is not in use.
2. Type ZAP and press RETURN.

    If SET SAFETY is ON, a screen prompt will ask if you really want to do this (Y/N). Press Y to proceed. Any open index files in the current work area are automatically zapped as well as the entire database file. ZAP is equivalent to DELETE ALL followed by PACK, but ZAP takes less time.

File Management

FILE STRUCTURE COMMANDS

Viewing the Structure of a File

1. Type USE <database filename> and press RETURN if the data file is not currently in use.
2. Type DISPLAY STRUCTURE and press RETURN.

   Note: The command LIST STRUCTURE is equivalent to the command DISPLAY STRUCTURE.

Copying the File Structure

A new file is created duplicating the fields of the original file when the file structure is copied. No data are copied to the newly created file.

1. Type USE <original filename> and press RETURN if the data file is not in use.
2. Type COPY TO <new database filename> STRUCTURE and press RETURN.
3. Type USE <new filename> and press RETURN.
4. Type DISPLAY STRUCTURE and press RETURN.

Modifying the File Structure

It is sometimes necessary to change or modify the structure of a file. The MODIFY STRUCTURE command automatically makes a backup copy of the original file structure, displays the copy on screen for the user to change, and appends the contents of the original file to the modified structure.

Caution: dBASE does *not* make a backup copy of the records in the file. *Always* make a backup copy of the file *before* modifying the structure.

There are certain limitations in modifying the structure of a file:

- fieldnames and field lengths should not be changed at the same time or data cannot be appended to the modified file structure. Use MODIFY STRUCTURE twice, change the fieldnames first and then change the field lengths.
- Data are not appended to the modified structure in fields that were changed from numeric to non-numeric field types. dBASE matches fieldnames from the original file to the file with the modified structure. Data are appended only in fields that have the same name, type, and length.
- No data are appended into a new field that is added when the structure is modified to include an additional field.

Changing the Structure of a File

1. Type USE <original filename> and press RETURN.
2. Type COPY STRUCTURE TO <new filename> and press RETURN.
3. Type USE <new filename> and press RETURN.
4. Type MODIFY STRUCTURE and press RETURN.
5. Enter changes into the file structure displayed.
6. Press CTRL and END (^END) when all changes have been entered.

   The modified structure is saved. Records from the original file are automatically appended to the modified structure.

7. Type DISPLAY STRUCTURE and press RETURN.
8. Type LIST OFF and press RETURN.

   The appended records and the modified structure are displayed on screen.

Exiting MODIFY STRUCTURE without Saving Changes

1. Press ESC.

Printing the Structure of the File

1. Type USE <database filename> and press RETURN if the data file is not currently in use.
2. Type DISPLAY STRUCTURE TO PRINT and press RETURN.

DATABASE FILE COMMANDS

Using Files

In dBASE the USE command opens a file.

Using a Database File

1. Type USE <database filename> and press RETURN.

Using One Index File with a Database File

1. Type USE <database filename> INDEX <index filename> and press RETURN.

Using Multiple Index Files with a Database File

1. Type USE <database filename> INDEX <index filename 1, index filename 2, ...> and press RETURN.

VIEWING FILES

Filenames and their file extensions (indicating the kind of file) can be displayed on screen as well as the contents (records) of a file.

Viewing the Contents of a Database File

1. Type USE <database filename> and press RETURN if the data file is not in use.
2. Type DISPLAY ALL and press RETURN.

   Note: The command DISPLAY ALL is equivalent to the command LIST. LIST does not pause periodically.

Viewing the Name of Files on the Default Disk Drive

1. Type DIR and press RETURN.

Viewing the Names of Data Files on Another Disk Drive

On a System without a Hard Disk

1. Type DIR B: and press RETURN.

   Note: The data disk must be located in disk drive B on a double disk drive system to issue this command.

On a System with a Hard Disk

1. Type DIR A: and press RETURN.

   Note: Hard disk users must have the data disk on which the file is stored in drive A to issue this command.

Viewing Specific Types of Files on a Given Disk Drive

   On a double disk drive system

1. Type DISPLAY FILES LIKE *.<file type> ON B and press RETURN.

   Note: File types are .dbf, .cmd, .fmt, .frm, .ndx, .prg, and

On a System with a Hard Disk

Hard disk users must have the data disk in drive A to issue this command.

1. Type DISPLAY FILES LIKE *.<file type> ON A and press RETURN.

Viewing All Files of All Types on a Given Disk Drive

On a Double Disk Drive System

1. Type LIST FILES ON B: LIKE *.* and press RETURN.

On a System with a Hard Disk

Hard disk users must have the data disk in drive A to issue this command.

1. Type LIST FILES ON A: LIKE *.* and press RETURN.

COPYING FILES

You should make backup copies of all database files on a regular basis. Data can be destroyed or damaged during a power failure, by a command entered in error, or because of other mishaps. Reentering lost data of a large database in time-consuming and costly. MAKE FREQUENT COPIES of your work.

Copying a Database File

The COPY TO command copies all records unless a scope qualifier is included in the command.

1. Type USE <original database filename> and press RETURN if the data file is not in use.
2. Type COPY TO <new filename> and press RETURN.

Copying Specified Fields to a New Database File

1. Type USE <original database filename> and press RETURN if the data file is not in use.
2. Type COPY TO <new filename> FIELDS < field 1, field 2, .., field n> and press RETURN.

Copying Fields That Match Specified Data

1. Type USE <original database filename> and press RETURN if the data file is not in use.
2. Type COPY TO <new filename> FIELDS <field 1, field 2, .., field n> FOR <fieldname> = '<data to be matched> ' and press RETURN.

   Example: COPY TO sales86 FIELDS dept, unit-price, quantity; FOR state = 'Michigan'

   Note: Anything within quotes must be exactly as it is in the file, including capital and lowercase letters.

Copying All Types of Files, Including Database Files

1. Type COPY FILE <original filename.extension> TO <new filename.extension> and press RETURN.

RENAMING FILES IN dBASE

Renaming a File on the Default Drive

1. Type RENAME <filename.extension> TO <new filename.extension> and press RETURN.

Renaming a File on a Drive Other Than the Default Drive

On a Double Disk Drive System

1. Type RENAME B: <filename.extension> TO B: <new filename.extension> and press RETURN.

On a Hard Disk System

1. Type RENAME A: <filename.extension> TO A: <new filename.extension> and press RETURN.

REMOVING FILES FROM A DIRECTORY WHILE IN dBASE

Removing a File from the Directory

1. Type ERASE < filename.extension> and press RETURN.

CLOSING FILES AND REMAINING IN dBASE

Closing a Database File Currently in Use

1. Type USE and press RETURN.

    The active file and index files in the current work area are closed.

Closing All Open Index Files of a Database File in Use

1. Type CLOSE INDEX and press RETURN.

    All open index files are closed. The database file is still open and currently the working file.

Closing All Open Database, Index, and Format Files

1. Type CLOSE DATABASES and press RETURN.

   All open database, index, and format files are closed, including those open but not in the current work area.

CLOSING FILES AND EXITING dBASE

Closing All Open Files and Returning to the Operating System

1. Type QUIT and press RETURN.

   All open files are closed, and you are returned to the operating system.

TEXT FILE COMMANDS

Viewing Contents of Text File

1. Type TYPE <filename.extension> and press RETURN.

   TYPE displays only standard ASCII files, not dBASE III files. TYPE does *not* display an open file.

   The filename must include the file extension and disk drive designation if the file is *not* on the default drive.

Printing Contents of a Text File

1. Type TYPE <filename.extension> TO PRINT and press RETURN.

Computation in dBASE

USING MATH FUNCTIONS

dBASE has commands that perform computation on numeric fields. You can COUNT, SUM, TOTAL, and AVERAGE numeric data, as well as add (+), subtract (-), multiply (*), and divide (/) the numeric data. The SUM and TOTAL commands are used to add numeric field data.

SUM totals numeric field data and displays the results on the screen.

TOTAL performs the same addition, but the results are saved in a new database file with the same key field as the original file. The new file has the same structure as the original file, with only one entry (the total) in each numeric field. The new Totals file can be used to save time when writing reports and when subtotals of fields are needed.

COUNT is the dBASE command that counts the number of records that match conditions requested by the user. The pointer location does not matter when the COUNT command is issued. The COUNT command automatically resets the pointer at the first record.

COUNTING RECORDS

The number of records that satisfy specified conditions can be counted. The user sometimes needs to know the number of records equal to, greater than, or less than some value or date.

Using COUNT to Determine the Number of Records That Meet Specified Conditions

1. Type USE <database filename> and press RETURN if the data file is not in use.
2. Type COUNT FOR <fieldname> = '<data to be matched>' and press RETURN.

   Example: COUNT FOR zipcode = '54157'

USING SUM

SUM totals data in numeric fields. It is possible to SUM more than one field at a time or to find the sum of two combined fields.

Using SUM to Total the Contents of One Field

1. Type USE <database filename> and press RETURN if the data file is not in use.
2. Type SUM <numeric fieldname> and press RETURN.

Using SUM to Total the Contents of Several Fields

1. Type USE <database filename> and press RETURN if the data file is not in use.
2. Type SUM <field 1, field 2, ... field n> and press RETURN.

   Each field is totaled, and the results for each field are displayed on screen.

Using SUM to Add the Contents of Two Combined Fields

1. Type USE <database filename> and press RETURN if the data file is not in use.
2. Type SUM <field 1 + field 2> TO <field 3> and press RETURN.

Using SUM to Calculate Total Price

Total price or total cost is calculated by multiplying two fields (Unit price and Quantity), then adding the results.

(Total Price = Unit price * Quantity)

The * is the computer symbol for multiplication.

1. Type USE <database filename> and press RETURN if the data file is not in use.
2. Type SUM <fieldname 1> * <fieldname 2> and press RETURN.

   Example: SUM unit-price*quantity

Using SUM to Calculate the Subtotal Cost of Specified Records

1. Type USE <database filename> and press RETURN if the data file is not in use.
2. Type SUM <fieldname 1> * <fieldname 2>; FOR <fieldname 3> = '<data to be matched> ' and press RETURN.

   Example: SUM unit-price*quantity FOR ITEM = 'pens'

Using SUM to Calculate the Subtotal for a Given Date

1. Type USE <database filename> and press RETURN if the data file is not in use.
2. Type SUM <fieldname 1> * <fieldname 2>; FOR DTOC(DATE) = '<date to be matched>' and press RETURN.

   Example: SUM unit-price*quantity FOR DTOC(DATE) = '05/14/86'

Using SUM to Calculate Totals on Fields Greater Than a Specified Amount

1. Type USE <database filename> and press RETURN if the data file is not in use.
2. Type SUM <fieldname 1> FOR <fieldname 1> >= 15 and press RETURN.

   Example: SUM sales FOR sales >= 15

Using SUM to Calculate Totals after a Given Date

1. Type USE <database filename> and press RETURN if the data file is not in use.
2. Type SUM <fieldname 1> FOR DTOC(DATE)> 'date to be matched' and press RETURN.

   Example: SUM sales FOR DTOC(DATE)>'07/07'

USING TOTAL

The TOTAL command works only on indexed or sorted database files. It is faster than using SUM when working on large databases. TOTAL works only on individual indexed fields. This command cannot perform calculations using two fields, such as TOTAL ON item TO itemsum FIELDS unit-price*quantity.

Using TOTAL to Calculate Subtotals

1. Type USE <database filename> and press RETURN if the data file is not in use.
2. Type SET INDEX TO <index filename> and press RETURN.

   The SET INDEX TO command is used if the file is already indexed on the appropriate key field.

   If the file is not already indexed, then index the file before totaling (INDEX ON <key fieldname> TO <index filename>) and press RETURN.

3. Type TOTAL ON <key fieldname> TO <new totals file> and press RETURN.

   Example: TOTAL ON sales TO salestot

4. Type USE <new totals filename> and press RETURN.
5. Type LIST and press RETURN.

   All numeric fields are totaled unless a scope qualifier is used with the TOTAL command. Only the indexed key field is displayed with LIST unless other fields are named in the LIST command.

Viewing Totals for Several Fields

5. Type LIST <field 1, field 2, ..., field n> and press RETURN.

    Only the fields listed are displayed on the screen.

USING AVERAGE

AVERAGE calculates the arithmetic mean of a group of numbers. In other words, dBASE III adds several numbers and divides the sum by the number of items added. All numeric fields are averaged unless a scope qualifier is included with the command.

Using AVERAGE to Average Numeric Fields

1. Type USE <database filename> and press RETURN if the data file is not in use.
2. Type AVERAGE <numeric fieldname> FOR <character fieldname> = 'data to be matched' and press RETURN.

    Example: AVERAGE sales FOR dept = 'stationery'

Reports

GENERATING REPORTS

Reports summarize information contained in the database file. The report information is displayed on screen and printed in a row and column format, one field per column, with a report heading (Title), date, and column(field) headings.

You need to determine which database files and which fields from those files are to be used to generate your report. You determine the report title (heading), column (field) headings, width of the columns, and whether or not pages are to be numbered.

Reports are created (generated) by the command CREATE REPORT. This command displays a series of screens: entry of titles and page format screen; group/subgroup totals screen; and the column design screen. If totals are not needed in the report, the second screen may be bypassed and the report is created using only the first and third screens.

Each screen displays the file structure of the database file in use across the top of the screen. The report being written is displayed, together with the screen prompts for data entry on the screen below the file structure.

The report is saved as a report form file (.frm). Database file commands are not used to change, view, or print report form files. MODIFY REPORT is the command used to change the format and/or contents of a report form file. REPORT FORM is the command used to display or print the contents of a report form file.

CREATE REPORT is a full screen command. The arrow keys and CTRL sequences are the same as those used in EDIT and other full screen commands. PgUp displays the preceding screen and PgDn displays the next screen. During the report generating process, it is possible to move back and forth from screen to screen and to change entered data.

Default Settings for Reports

Left margin	8 characters
	0 characters if report is to be viewed on the screen only
Page length	58 lines
Page width	80 characters

Creating a Report

1. Type USE <database filename> and press RETURN if the data file is not in use.
2. Type CREATE REPORT <report filename> and press RETURN.
3. Type <report title> and press CTRL END (^END) to move the cursor to the printing specifications.

   The arrow keys can be used to move the cursor on the screen.

4. Enter the values for page width, left margin, and right margin and type Y or N to double-space the report.
5. Press PgDn or RETURN to move to the next screen.

   The second screen is to be completed if you want subtotals. You have the option of setting up the report initially without sub totals. You can modify the report to include subtotals after you have designed your basic report format.

6. Press CTRL PgDn (*cflex*PgDn) to move to the third screen (column design).

   A report column can contain more than one field.

   The report column width does not have to be the same width as the original data field. The report column can be wider than the data field, but do not make the report column less than the field width.

   Each column may contain up to four lines of 60 characters/line

You will be prompted for the following information:
- Name of data field that contains the information to be used in the first column of the report
- Field contents
- Column heading or field header
- Width of output column

7. Type the fieldname, field contents, field header, and width of the output column and press RETURN.

   It is not necessary to enter the width of each field. dBASE III will automatically assign the larger of the field width or heading width as the column width in the report. If you change the width, increase it.

8. Repeat step 7 for each column to be included in the report.

Exiting CREATE REPORT

1. Press CTRL END (^END) to stop the process when prompted for a new column width and contents.

   You are returned to the dot prompt of dBASE. The report form is saved.

   Note: If the dot prompt (.) does not appear on screen, press the NUM LOCK key once and CTRL END.(^END)

CREATING REPORTS WITH TOTALS

Creating a Report with Subtotals on a Field

The database file must be indexed on the fields to be subtotaled when you first begin.

1. Type USE <database filename> INDEX <key field> and press RETURN.
2. Type CREATE REPORT <report filename> and press RETURN.

   Note: dBASE III permits entry of two levels of subtotals. Subtotals work correctly only on data fields that have been indexed or sorted on the subtotal fields.

3. Type N to indicate that a full report, including individual items, is wanted. The summary report response Y would list subtotals only without any individual items.
4. Type N to indicate that you do not want to start a new page after each subtotal at the Eject prompt.

5. Type <heading> at the group/subtotal heading prompt.

Viewing a Report

1. Type REPORT FORM <report filename> and press RETURN.

Viewing Selected Records in a Report

1. Type REPORT FORM <report filename FOR <fieldname> = 'data to be matched and press RETURN.

Viewing Selected Records in a Report by Date

1. Type REPORT FORM <report filename> FOR DTOC(DATE) = 'mm/dd/yy and press RETURN.

Rearranging Data in a Report Using an Indexed File

1. Type USE <database filename> and press RETURN.
2. Type SET INDEX TO <index filename> and press RETURN.
3. Type REPORT FORM <report filename> and press RETURN.

Changing Data in a Report File

1. Type MODIFY REPORT <report filename> and press RETURN.
2. Press PgDn to view the screen containing the data to be changed.

If you know which screen contains the data to be changed:

2. Press CTRL and HOME (^HOME).

You will be prompted to select the appropriate screen.

Inserting Spaces in Front of a Report Column Heading

Sometimes it is necessary to widen report columns. This procedure moves a column to the right, widening the preceding column.

1. Type MODIFY REPORT <report filename> and press RETURN.
2. Press CTRL and HOME (^HOME) and select the screen that contains the column definition for the field to be widened.
3. Press RETURN.

The screen containing the column width to be changed should be displayed on screen.

4. Press INS once to turn on the insert mode.
5. Position the cursor under the first letter of the field contents to be shifted to the right.
6. Type ' '+ (Enter the appropriate number of blanks between the ').

   Warning: Do not press RETURN.

   The number of blank spaces entered in step 6 moves the data in the report column a corresponding number of spaces in the report.
7. Position the cursor at the field header.
8. Type the number of spaces necessary to reposition the column heading.
9. Press CTRL and END (^END).

Printing Reports

1. Type REPORT FORM <report filename> TO PRINT and press RETURN.

Multiple Files

MULTIPLE FILES IN dBASE III

You may have up to ten database files open (in USE) simultaneously. Each file in use can be used as if it were the only file open.

Each open file has its own assigned work area, identified as 1 through 10. Work area 1 is selected when dBASE III is entered. A separate work area must be identified and selected as each database file is opened in order to work with multiple files.

Once a file is opened in a work area, you move between work areas and files by selecting the work area number or by using the file to work with.

It is possible to move back and forth between open files by typing SELECT N when there is more than one file open at the same time. When work on the current (selected) file is done, SELECT another file and proceed to work on that file.

Each work area maintains a separate record pointer. dBASE III moves the pointer only in the SELECTed database file, even though more than one file is open. Only the active database file is affected by commands that change the position of the record pointer unless the SET RELATION TO command is used. The position of any record pointer is not affected by moving between work areas.

All normal database operations can be performed within the selected (active) file. The current record in any of the other files may be read but not changed while one file is worked on.

Using Multiple Files

1. Type USE < filename 1> and press RETURN.

   The first file opened is assigned work area 1 by dBASE III.

2. Type SELECT n and press RETURN.

   n is any unassigned work area through 10, not including 1, which is already in use.

3. Type USE <filename 2> and press RETURN.

   Filename 2 uses work area n.

   Example: USE CUSTOMERS and press RETURN.

   SELECT 2 and press RETURN.

   USE INVENTORY and press RETURN.

Moving between Open Database Files

1. Type SELECT 1 or SELECT <filename 1> and press RETURN.

   Note: Work areas may be designated by the numbers 1 through 10 or by the letters A through J.

2. Enter the commands necessary to accomplish the work on the active file.
3. Type SELECT 2 or SELECT <filename 2> and press RETURN.
4. Enter the commands necessary to accomplish the work on the active file.

Retrieving Data from Both Databases Simultaneously

5. Type filename 1 <- field 1, filename 1 <- field 2, filename 2 <- field 1 and press RETURN.

   The filename followed by <- before the fieldname tells dBASE III which file the field should be taken from.

   Example:

   SELECT 1 and press RETURN.

   LOCATE FOR PARTNO = '35-00-0001' and press RETURN.

   SELECT 2 and press RETURN.

DISPLAY ALL FOR PARTNO = '35-00-0001' and press RETURN.

customer <- custname,customer <- state,inventory <- quantity and press RETURN.

Closing Multiple Open Database Files

1. Type CLOSE DATA and press RETURN.

or

1. Type SELECT 1 and press RETURN.
2. Type USE and press RETURN.
3. Type SELECT 2 and press RETURN.
4. Type USE and press RETURN.

   Warning: Only the SELECTED database file is closed. Typing USE only one time does *not* close all open files in work areas.

Converting Files

FILE CONVERSION

dBASE III converts dBASE files into and accepts two ASCII formats :

Delimited: Commas or blanks separate fields, and delimiters (such as double quotes) enclose character fields.

SDF (system data format): Fixed length fields; carriage return and line feed separate records.

Note: Always make a backup copy of any file *before* converting it.

Converting a dBASE III File for Use with WordStar

Convert the dBASE III file to a SDF file.

1. Type USE <database filename> and press RETURN.
2. Type SET ALTERNATE TO MOVEFILE and press RETURN.
3. Type SET ALTERNATE ON and press RETURN.
4. Type REPORT FORM <database filename> and press RETURN.
5. Type SET ALTERNATE OFF and press RETURN.
6. Type CLOSE ALTERNATE and press RETURN.
7. Type QUIT and press RETURN.

8. Run the WordStar program.
9. Press CTRL KR and type MOVEFILE.TXT. Press RETURN to read the dBASE III converted file into a WS text file.
10. Edit as in any other WS text file.

Converting a dBASE III File for Use in MailMerge

1. Type USE <database filename> and press RETURN.
2. Type COPY TO WSMAIL.MRG DELIMITED WITH " and press RETURN.

The file is now in the format used by MailMerge.

Converting a dBASE III File for Use with SuperCalc3

Verify that your version of SuperCalc includes a utility program named SDI (SuperCalc Data Interchange).

SuperCalc requires that character fields begin with double quotation marks. Numeric fields cannot have quotation marks as the first character entry.

dBASE III fields must be divided into two groups: character fields and numeric fields. Each set of fields is copied to a separate database file before converting the files to SDI format acceptable to SuperCalc.

1. Type USE <database filename> and press RETURN.
2. Type COPY TO CHARFILE.CSV FIELDS <fieldname 1, fieldname 2, fieldname 3>DELIMITED WITH " and press RETURN.
3. Type COPY TO NUMFILE.CSV FIELDS <fieldname4, fieldname5> DELIMITED WITH , and press RETURN.
4. Replace the dBASE III system disk with the SuperCalc disk that contains the program SDI. Run SDI.
5. Read the CHARFILE.CSV file and then read the NUMFILE.CSV file.
6. Run SuperCalc3, load, and read the first file.
7. When loading the second file, specify Load/Part and the range it occupies so that both files may be loaded into the SuperCalc worksheet at once.

Converting a dBASE III File for Use with Lotus 1-2-3

Convert the dBASE III file to ASCII format as follows:

1. Type USE <database filename> and press RETURN.
2. Type COPY TO LOTUS.PRN DELIMITED and press RETURN.
3. Type /FS to save the ASCII format file and press RETURN.
4. Type < filename.prn> in the form the file is to saved as a LOTUS 1-2-3 file and press RETURN.

5. Determine where you wish to place the text in the spreadsheet.
6. Position the screen pointer in the upper left corner of the area in which the text is to be placed.
7. Type /F1 to select the File Import command and press RETURN.
8. Position the screen pointer on the format to be used.

IMPORTING FILES INTO dBASE III

Importing Files from WordStar

1. Type APPEND FROM <WordStar file.txt> DELIMITED WITH ' and press RETURN.

Importing Files from Lotus 1-2-3

Lotus 1-2-3 files must be translated to ASCII format before using them with dBASE III. Review the Lotus file and verify the following:

- all labels that will be used as fieldnames in the database file are no more than ten characters in length;
- all labels that will be used as fieldnames begin with an alphabetical letter;
- all labels that will be used as fieldnames contain no special characters (except a colon, which is acceptable);
- all dates have been converted to dd/mm/yy format before translating the Lotus 1-2-3 file.

Translating a Lotus 1-2-3 File

1. Position the cursor at the Lotus Access System (Opening) Menu.
2. Select the Utilities option and press RETURN.
3. Remove the Lotus system disk from the disk drive and replace it with the Lotus Utilities disk.
4. Position the pointer on Translate Utility and press RETURN.
5. Position the pointer on worksheet WKS TO DBF and press RETURN.
6. Position the pointer on the worksheet to translate the entire worksheet and press RETURN.

    If only a portion of the worksheet is to be translated, position the pointer on Range, press ENTER, type the range to be translated, and press RETURN.

7. Position the pointer on the file to be translated and press RETURN.
8. Type the disk drive on which the translated file is to be stored and press RETURN.

9. Type Y (yes) to translate the file and press RETURN.
10. Type Q or position the pointer on QUIT to leave the Translate Menu and press RETURN.

    When in dBASE III:
11. Create a database with fieldnames that match the Lotus 1-2-3 fieldnames.
12. Type APPEND FROM <Lotus filename> WKS and press RETURN.

Using Function Keys

FUNCTION KEYS

Function keys (F1–F10) are located on the left-hand side of the keyboard or across the top of the keyboard. dBASE III has assigned certain dBASE commands to these function keys.

FUNCTION KEY ASSIGNMENTS

F1	HELP
F2	ASSIST (makes all commands menu-driven). A database file must be open to use any of the menu features.
F3	LIST (DISPLAY ALL)
F4	DIR (LIST FILES)
F5	LIST STRUCTURE (DISPLAY STRUCTURE)
F6	LIST STATUS (DISPLAY MEMORY)
F7	LIST MEMORY (DISPLAY MEMORY)
F8	DISPLAY
F9	APPEND
F10	EDIT

REPROGRAMMING A FUNCTION KEY

Any function key except F1 can be temporarily reprogrammed for the duration of a dBASE III session.

1. Type USE <database filename> and press RETURN.
2. Type SET FUNCTION n TO " <command used frequently> ;" and press RETURN.

   Example: SET FUNCTION 2 TO "SUM HOURS * PAYRATE TO WAGES;" and press RETURN.

   Note: With the semicolon in the command, dBASE III executes the command without waiting for the user to press RETURN after pressing the function key.

   The semicolon should be omitted if additional information must be entered before the command is executed after pressing the function key.

CHANGING A FUNCTION KEY PERMANENTLY

1. Type MODIFY COMMAND CONFIG.DB and press RETURN.
2. Type F2 = <command used frequently> and press RETURN.
3. Press CTRL and END to exit the dBASE editor and save the changes in the CONFIG.DB file.

New Features of dBASE III PLUS

CHANGES AND NEW FEATURES OF dBASE III PLUS

dBASE III PLUS has new features and has made changes since dBASE III Version 1.1. The new features outlined below are those all users of dBASE will find useful. The new programming commands are not included in this listing.

The dBASE commands that are now fully menu-driven with a user-friendly interface are ASSIST, CREATE/MODIFY LABEL, CREATE/MODIFY QUERY, CREATE/MODIFY REPORT, CREATE/MODIFY SCREEN, CREATE/MODIFY VIEW, and SET. The Assistant is the user interface that permits users to quickly create and build databases, set up relationships in view files, specify the scope of queries, and perform familiar database operations. The Assistant appears on screen when dBASE III PLUS is booted.

Escaping The Assistant to the Dot Prompt

1. Press the ESC key when the main menu heading is displayed.

NEW COMMANDS

CREATE/MODIFY QUERY: Creates or changes a query file.

CREATE/MODIFY SCREEN: Creates or changes a screen file and the format file associated with it.

CREATE/MODIFY VIEW: Creates or changes a view file.

EXPORT: Converts a dBASE III PLUS database and related format file to a pfs:File format.

IMPORT: Converts a pfs:File file to a dBASE III PLUS database format and view file.

SET FIELDS ON/OFF: Determines whether all fields or only fields in the field pool are used with commands such as EDIT or LIST.

SET FIELDS TO: Automatically toggles SET FIELDS ON and adds fields to the field pool.

SET FILTER TO FILE: Opens a query file and activates the stored filter to limit the fields displayed.

SET ORDER TO: Changes the order of the open index files to make the specified index file the active one.

Example: SET ORDER TO 2 The second index file opened is now the active index file.

SET VIEW TO: Activates a view file.

NEW NUMERIC FUNCTIONS

ABS(): Displays the absolute value of a number.

MAX(): Determines the greater of two numbers.

MIN: Determines the lesser of two numbers.

MOD: Displays the remainder when the arithmetic operation of division is performed.

NEW FUNCTIONS

DBF(): Displays the name of the database file in the active work area.

DISKSPACE(): Displays how many bytes are available on the default disk drive.

FIELD(): Displays the fieldname that corresponds to the the number entered in the command.

Example: FIELD(3) displays the name of the third field.

FOUND(): Displays T, a logical True if a record is located when a FIND, LOCATE, or SEEK command is issued.

LUPDATE(): Displays the date of the last update to a database file.

NDX(): Displays the names of the open index files in an active work area.

OS(): Displays the name and version of the operating system.

READKEY(): Determines the last full-screen editing key pressed.

RECOUNT(): Displays the number of records in the database file (eliminates the need to type GOTO BOTTOM).

RECSIZE(): Displays the size in bytes of a database record.

VERSION(): Displays the dBASE III PLUS version name and number.

NEW STRING FUNCTIONS

ISALPHA(): Evaluates the first character of a string to determine if it is a letter.

ISLOWER(): Evaluates the first character of a string to determine if it is a lower case letter.

ISUPPER(): Evaluates the first character of a string to determine if it is an upper case letter.

LEFT(): Searches for a substring from the left end of a character string.

LTRIM: Removes leading blanks in a string.

RTRIM(): Removes trailing blanks in a string.

REPLICATE(): Allows repetition of a string.

STUFF(): Allows the user to insert, remove, or replace characters in a string.

TRANSFORM(): Allows use of PICTURE clauses when the commands DISPLAY, LIST, and REPLACE are used to view data or when generating reports.

The Assistant

USING THE ASSISTANT

The Assistant is a collection of menus that can be used to set up a database quickly. By using The Assistant it is possible to set up a database, enter and add data, edit entries, delete entries, find data, index and sort data, save a database, and print simple database files.
    Creating query files to locate and print specified records, creating custom data entry forms, and printing custom forms are new features of dBASE III Plus. These features can be accessed through The Assistant or by commands entered at the dot prompt.
    Features such as modifying database file structures, backing up files, and quitting dBASE III Plus are also accessed through the menus of The Assistant as well as as by commands entered at the dot prompt.
    Using multiple files simultaneously and joining database files are not features available through The Assistant. The commands to select different files and work areas and to join files are entered at the dot prompt.

ENTERING dBASE III PLUS

The dBASE III Plus Assistant appears on screen when dBASE is invoked.

1. Type dBASE at the operating system prompt and press RETURN.

   The Assistant menu selections are displayed at the top of the screen along with several status/information lines at the bottom of the screen.

FEATURES OF THE ASSISTANT DISPLAY

The Assistant display consists of menus displayed in the top portion of the screen and status/instruction lines displayed at the bottom of the screen.

Top Portion of the Screen Display Consists of:

- The menu selections displayed at the top of the screen (Set Up, Create, Update, Position, Retrieve, Organize, Modify, and Tools)
- Pull-down menu options that are displayed below the selected highlighted menu heading
- Submenus that are displayed next to the pull-down menu options list

Bottom Portion of the Screen Display Consists of:

- The Command in Use line, which is the top line of the bottom screen display
- The Status Bar, which indicates if The Assistant is in use (ASSIST), the current disk drive in use, the name of the database file in use, the number of records in the file, and the first record number
- The status of the INS (insert), CAPS LOCK, and NUM LOCK keys (all should be OFF)
- The navigation line (second from the bottom of the screen display), which informs the user how to use the current menu display
- The message line (bottom line of the screen display), which describes the current operation and the entry to be made next

USING MENUS

Opening the Selected Menu

1. Press the left or right arrow key to move from one menu selection to another. The selected menu is highlighted.

   or

1. Type the first letter of the menu selection desired.

A pull-down list of menu options is displayed on screen for the highlighted menu selection.

Selecting Menu Options

1. Press the up and down arrow keys to highlight a menu option.
2. Press RETURN to select the highlighted option.

   Note: To use menu options for headings other than SET UP and CREATE, you must already have an existing database file. If the database file does not already exist, you must CREATE a file before using any of the other menu selection headings.

Selecting Submenu Options

A submenu is displayed next to the menu options list when the Menu Option is selected by pressing RETURN.
   You are asked to select the disk drive on which the database file is located.

1. Press the up arrow or down arrow key to move within the submenu, highlighting the selected item.
2. Press RETURN to select the highlighted item.

   A list of existing database files is displayed.

3. Press the up and down arrow keys to highlight the file and to scroll additional files into display.
4. Press RETURN to select a highlighted file.

Canceling Selections

1. Press the ESC (escape) key to cancel a selection.

   You are returned to the previous level menu selection.

EXITING THE ASSISTANT

Escaping The Assistant to the Dot Prompt of dBASE III Plus

1. Continue to press the ESC key until you are returned to the main menu heading selections.
2. Press ESC to leave The Assistant and run the program from the dot prompt.

Returning to The Assistant from the Dot Prompt

1. At the dot prompt, type assist and press RETURN.

   or

1. Press the F2 (function) key.

Quitting dBASE III Plus from The Assistant

1. Open the Set Up Menu, using the right and left arrow keys to highlight the Set Up Menu, or type S.
2. Use the up and down arrow keys to highlight QUIT dBASE III PLUS and press RETURN.

CONVERTING FILES

Conversion of dBASE III Plus Files to pfs:File Files

1. Open the TOOLS menu and select EXPORT in the list of menu options. Complete the conversion from dBASE III Plus files to pfs:File files as prompted by The Assistant.

Conversion of pfs:File Files to dBASE III Plus Files

1. Open the TOOLS menu and select IMPORT in the list of menu options. Complete the conversion from pfs:FILE files to dBASE III Plus files as prompted by The Assistant.

   Note: The dBASE commands APPEND FROM used to convert ASCII and SDF files to dBASE III or dBASE III Plus files and the COPY TO used to convert dBASE III and III Plus files to ASCII text files are not available from The Assistant.

THE QUERY OPTION

The QUERY option lets you create a .qry file, which can be used to limit the information displayed. Only records that meet specified conditions are displayed when commands are issued after the query file is set up.

The query file can be created and modified by selecting the Create menu heading.

VIEW FILES

The CREATE VIEW command is used to create a view file that contains a database file, the index files associated with the database file, the work area selections for each of these files, relations between files if more than one database file is selected, and the currently selected work area. The view file may also contain selected fields from each database file, a format file, and a filter condition that determines which records will be displayed.

View files may also be created by using The Assistant and selecting the Create menu heading.

LICENSE AGREEMENT AND DISCLAIMER

A version of this manual contains an educational version of dBASE III PLUS. Using the diskette(s) accompanying the manual indicates your acceptance of the terms and conditions outlined below:

The Software is protected by copyright laws, and no unauthorized copying, distribution of, or any other act with respect to the Software is allowed that would violate those laws. You may not modify, reverse engineer, decompile, or disassemble the Software and may not deliver copies to, or sell, rent, lease, or sublicense the Software to anyone else.

Addison-Wesley warrants that the diskette(s) delivered are free from defects in materials and faulty workmanship under normal use during the period of 90 days from the date of original delivery. If a defect in a diskette appears during this 90-day period, the defective item may be returned to Addison-Wesley, postage prepaid, addressed to Micromatters Marketing, Addison-Wesley Publishing Company, Route 128, Reading, MA 01867. Addison-Wesley will replace the defective item without charge. This warranty applies only to diskettes packaged with this manual and does not cover items damaged, modified, or misused after delivery.

This warranty is in lieu of all other express warranties on the diskette(s). The software itself is licensed "as is," without any express or implied warranties whatsoever. The owners, their distributors, and dealers shall in no event be liable for any indirect, incidental, or consequential damages, whether resulting from defects in the diskette(s) or from any defect in the software itself or documentation thereof.

Any implied warranties that are found to exist are hereby limited in duration to the 90-day life of the express warranties on the diskette(s) given above. Some states do not allow the exclusion or limitation of incidental or consequential damages, or any limitation on how long implied warranties last, so these exclusions or limitations may not apply to you. This warranty gives you specific legal rights and you may also have other rights, which vary from state to state.